Implementing
Response-to-Intervention
in Elementary and
Secondary Schools

School-Based Practice in Action Series

Series Editors
Rosemary B. Mennuti, Ed.D., NCSP
and
Ray W. Christner, Psy.D., NCSP
Philadelphia College of Osteopathic Medicine

This series provides school-based practitioners with concise practical guidebooks that are designed to facilitate the implementation of evidence-based programs into school settings, putting the best practices *in action*.

Published Titles

Implementing Response-to-Intervention in Elementary and Secondary Schools: Procedures to Assure Scientific-Based Practices
Matthew K. Burns and Kimberly Gibbons

Forthcoming Titles

Assessment and Intervention for Executive Function Difficulties
George McCloskey, Lisa A. Perkins, and Bob Van Divner

Resilient Playgrounds
Beth Doll and Katherine Brehm

Implementing Response-to-Intervention in Elementary and Secondary Schools

Procedures to Assure Scientific-Based Practices

Matthew K. Burns ■ Kimberly Gibbons

Routledge
Taylor & Francis Group
New York   London

MT

Routledge
Taylor & Francis Group
270 Madison Avenue
New York, NY 10016

Routledge
Taylor & Francis Group
2 Park Square
Milton Park, Abingdon
Oxon OX14 4RN

International Standard Book Number-13: 978-0-415-96392-3 (Softcover) 978-0-415-96391-6 (0)

Library of Congress Cataloging-in-Publication Data

Burns, Matthew K.
  Implementing response-to-intervention in primary and secondary schools : procedures to assure scientific-based practices / Matthew K. Burns, Kimberly Gibbons.
      p. cm. -- (School based practice in action series)
  Includes bibliographical references and index.
  ISBN-13: 978-0-415-96392-3 (softcover)
  ISBN-13: 978-0-415-96391-6 (hardcover) 1. Remedial teaching. 2. Learning disabled children--Education. I. Gibbons, Kimberly. II. Title.

  LB1029.R4B78 2008
  371.9'043--dc22   2007030771

Visit the Taylor & Francis Web site at
http://www.taylorandfrancis.com

and the Routledge Web site at
http://www.routledge.com

10/13/09

Contents

List of Tables and Figures

TABLES

FIGURES

Series Editors' Foreword

The *School-Based Practice in Action* series grew out of the coming together of our passion and commitment to the field of education and the needs of children and schools in today's world. We entered the process of developing and editing this series at two different points of our careers, though both in phases of transition. One (Ray W. Christner) moving from the opening act to the main scene and the other (Rosemary B. Mennuti) from the main scene to the final act. Despite one of us entering the peak of action and the other leaving it, we both continue to be faced with the same challenges in and visions for education and serving children and families.

Significant transformations to the educational system, through legislation such as the No Child Left Behind Act and the reauthorization of the Individuals with Disabilities Education Improvement Act (2004), have had broad sweeping changes for the practitioners in the educational setting, and these changes will likely continue. It is imperative that as school-based practitioners we maintain a strong knowledge base and adjust our service delivery. To accomplish this, there is a need to understand theory and research, but it is critical that we have the resources to move our empirical knowledge into the process of practice. Thus, it is our goal that the books included in the *School-Based Practice in Action* series truly offer resources for readers to put directly "into action."

To accomplish this, each book in the series will offer information in a practice-friendly manner and will have a companion CD with reproducible and usable materials. Within the text, readers will find a specific icon that will cue them to documents available on the accompanying compact disk. These resources are designed to have a direct impact on transitioning research and knowledge into the day-to-day functions of school-based practitioners. We recognize that the implementation of programs and the changing of roles come with challenges and barriers and, as such, these may take on various forms depending on the context of the situation and the voice of the practitioner. To that end, the books of this series may be used in their entirety and present form by a number of practitioners; however, for others, these books will help them find new ways to move toward effective action and new possibilities. No matter which style fits your practice, we hope that these books will influence your work and professional growth.

To start our series, we are pleased to have had the opportunity to work with Dr. Matt Burns and Dr. Kim Gibbons, who have developed an outstanding guidebook on an issue that remains at the center of education: response-to-intervention (RTI). Although several excellent books exist on RTI (see Jimerson, Burns, and VanDerHeyden's *Handbook of Response to Intervention: The Science and Practice of Assessment and Intervention*, 2007; and Brown-Chidsey and Steege's *Response to Intervention: Principles and Strategies for Effective Practice*, 2005), Burns and Gibbons have compiled a resource moving the knowledge base from the discussion of RTI to detailed and systematic recommendations to enhance the implementation of RTI services. This book is grounded in their wisdom and practical experience. Not only do they offer a book that provides a foundation in understanding RTI, but they also offer key points and usable materials that will facilitate the readers' skills in developing effective services for children and schools.

Finally, we want to extend our gratitude to Mr. Dana Bliss and the publisher Routledge for their support and vision in developing a book series focused on enriching the practice and service delivery within school settings. Their openness to meeting the needs of school-based practitioners has made the *School-Based Practice in Action* series possible. We hope that you enjoy reading and implementing the materials in this book and the rest of the series as much as we have enjoyed working with the authors on developing these resources.

Rosemary B. Mennuti, Ed.D., NCSP

Ray W. Christner, Psy.D., NCSP
Series Editors, School-Based Practice in Action

Acknowledgments

The authors gratefully acknowledge the teachers, support staff, and administrators of the St. Croix River Education District in Minnesota for their work and perseverance in implementing response-to-intervention (RTI), which was the basis for much of what was included in this book. We also acknowledge our appreciation for the patience and loving support of our families, Mary Beth, Matthew, and Kathleen Burns and Aaron, Eli, Zachary, and Isabella Gibbons. Finally, we thank Dr. Ray Christner and Dr. Rosemary Mennuti for their editorial contributions to this book and for their leadership in the *School-Based Practice in Action* series.

This book is dedicated to all of those thankless professionals who pioneered RTI decades ago and who continue to implement it today. Sometimes what is best for children is not what is easiest for the adults who serve them, but they persevere with the best interests of others in mind.

Abbreviations

BEA	brief experimental analysis
CBM	curriculum-based measurement
CBM-R	curriculum-based measures of reading
CD	compact disk
DD	dually discrepant
DIBELS	Dynamic Indicators of Basic Early Literacy Skills
EBASS	Ecobehavior Assessment System Software
ELL	English language learner
FAAB	Functional Assessment of Academic Behavior
FRL	federal free or reduced lunch
GOMs	general outcome measures
ICEL	instructional, curricular, environmental, and learner
IDEA	Indivudals with Disabilities Education Act
IEP	individual education plan
IQ	intelligence quotient
IRLD	Institute for Research on Learning Disabilities
LD	learning disabled
MCA	Minnesota Comprehensive Assessment
NCLB	No Child Left Behind [Act]
NRP	National Reading Panel
ORF	oral reading fluency
PALS	peer-assisted learning strategies
PBS	positive behavior support
PII	problem identification interview
P.L.	public law
PSM	problem-solving model
PST	problem-solving team
RAF	request for assistance form
RIOT	review, interview, observe, test
RTI	response-to-intervention
SAT	student assistant team
SBR	scientifically research based
SCRED	St. Croix River Education District
SLD	specific learning disability
SMM	subskill mastery measure
SST	student support team

STEEP   System to Enhance Educational Performance
TAT   teacher assistance team
WRC   words read correctly
WRCM words read correctly per minute

1

Response-to-Intervention:
What It Is and Why We Do It

The title of this chapter may sound familiar to many because it is an intentional paraphrase of Marston's (1989) chapter in Shinn's curriculum-based measurement (CBM) book. The reason for this paraphrasing is because much of the basis for response-to-intervention, CBM, and many current initiatives in education can be traced to the work on data-based decision making by Deno and Mirkin (1977) and the U.S. Department of Education's report *A Nation at Risk* (1983). It seems that data-based decision making is a concept whose time has come in education, but it has been a long time coming.

Response-to-intervention (RTI) is the systematic use of assessment data to most efficiently allocate resources in order to improve learning for all students (Burns & VanDerHeyden, 2006). Thus, it is the latest installment of the data-based decision-making movement that began with Bloom, Hastings, and Madaus's (1971) seminal work on formative assessment, which was then further operationalized by Deno and Mirkin (1977). However, the recent federal provision for RTI was the culmination of years of events that affected how RTI is conceptualized today. Therefore, the goal of this first chapter is to discuss how we got here, what RTI is, and what happens when RTI is implemented.

HOW WE GOT HERE

The 2004 reauthorization of the Individuals with Disabilities Education Improvement Act states that a local education agency "may use a process that determines if the child responds to scientific, research-based intervention as a part of the evaluation procedures" (P.L. No. 108-446 § 614 [b][6][A]; § 614 [b] [2 & 3]). That relatively simple sentence is the basis for a great deal of change, possibility, and controversy, but it did not start there. The role of the federal government in funding special education, dissatisfaction with special education, increased knowledge of learning and academic interventions, and the accountability movement in this country have all contributed to RTI's development and popularity, and they all need to be discussed to understand the direction and promise of RTI.

The Role of the Federal Government in Funding Special Education

When the Individuals with Disabilities Education Act (IDEA) was first made into law, it was expected that the federal government would fund 40% of the excess cost of providing special education services. The current federal share of the cost is approximately 17%. According to former assistant secretary of education Robert Pasternack, it is estimated that soon the federal government will spend $80 billion annually on special education in the upcoming year and 60% of students receiving special education services will be served under one category: specific learning disability. With that information in mind, prior to the 2004 IDEA reauthorization, the federal government was extremely interested in examining ways to prevent students from experiencing significant academic failure. RTI emerged as a viable method for preventing academic failure and reducing the learning disablility prevalence rate through universal screening for achievement difficulties, early intervention and prevention programs, and accountability for results through frequent progress monitoring.

Dissatisfaction with Special Education

Special education has been controversial since it was first mandated in 1975 (Ysseldyke, Algozzine, & Thurlow, 2000) due in large part to debates regarding the diagnostic procedures. Federal regulations for Public Law 94-142 were approved in 1977 as the Education of All Handicapped Children Act and included the now infamous discrepancy model in which children were identified with a learning disability (LD) only if there was a severe underachievement as compared to the child's intelligence. This definition of LD was the result of a compromise because there was no widely accepted or supported diagnostic model in 1977 (Gresham et al., 2004). Shortly after the regulations obtained the power of law, the Office of Special Education Programs at the U.S. Department of Education funded the Institute for Research on Learning Disabilities (IRLD) at the University of Minnesota to study LD diagnostic practices. Research from the IRLD quickly began questioning the model in place in federal and state regulations, but the funding and subsequent research occurred *after* the model was enacted.

Today there is consensus (Aaron, 1997; Fletcher et al., 1998) that the discrepancy model failed, but simply considering RTI as the contemporary LD diagnostic model does not tell the entire story. Meta-analytic research by Kavale and Forness (1999) has found small average effects for commonly used instructional approaches in special education such as perceptual training, matching a child's modality, and psycholinguistic training. Moreover, the average effect size for special education in general was -.12. This means that children with disabilities who did not receive special education actually outperformed their counterparts who did! However, large effect sizes for children identified as LD were found for somewhat less commonly used instructional approaches such as explicit comprehension instruction, direct instruction, and mnemonic strategies. These data suggested quite a bit of variance in student learning associated with the instructional approach used.

Finally, what is *special education*? It was originally defined, and continues to be so in the 2004 version of the IDEA, as "specially designed instruction, at no cost to the parents or guardians, to meet the unique needs of a child with a disability" (§ 300.39). Unfortunately, education in this country focused more on the "at no cost" component than specially designed instruction or the unique needs of a child with a disability. RTI is a direct attempt to return to the basis of special education by monitoring student response to instructional approaches, modifying those approaches based on the data in order to address the unique needs of each child, and to perhaps reach a more useful diagnosis of learning disability.

Knowledge of Human Learning and Interventions

Research on student learning has greatly enhanced the knowledge base from which we practice. Meta-analytic research has identified several effective practices for struggling learners with and without disabilities (Kavale & Forness, 1999; Swanson, Hoskyn, & Lee, 1999). Perhaps more important is a line of research demonstrating the physiological effects of effective interventions. Simos et al. (2002) studied a group of children who were diagnosed as LD *and* who matched the brain activation pattern while reading of children who are LD. Children with learning disabilities tend to focus on the right hemisphere of the brain while reading, or have no clear pattern. Skilled readers tend to focus their neurological activity on the left hemisphere of the brain, where language functions are centered. Simos et al. implemented an intervention with a strong research base and then repeated the imaging of the children while reading and found that the activity pattern had *normalized*. What this study demonstrated is that although we tend to focus on changing "brain chemistry" to change behavior, modifying behavior changes the chemistry and is the more plausible option in our schools. Needless to say, RTI is an attempt to improve learning by changing the behavior for individual children rather than following a traditional line of diagnosis to treatment.

The Accountability Movement

The *Nation at Risk* report (U.S. Department of Education, 1983) led to dramatic changes in American education by emphasizing a need for educational reform and leading to an increased interest in educational accountability (Ravitch, 1999). Salvia and Ysseldyke have defined *accountability* as documentation for people in authority that "desired goals are being met" (2001, p. 644). Prior to the amendments to the IDEA in 1997, desired goals were not specified for children with disabilities, but that changed when it was mandated that children who participated in special education participate in state accountability tests.

Although RTI was born in special education law, it was conceived in the No Child Left Behind Act (NCLB) of 2001. NCLB requires the measuring of the educational skills and progress of all children, including those with disabilities, those for whom English is not their native language, and those from low socioeconomic backgrounds. This emphasis on measuring student learning is consistent with the data-based decision-making movement that began in the 1970s and was endorsed by the President's Commission on Excellence in Special Education (2002) because "those that get counted, count." As a result, the 2004 version of the IDEA specifies that children could be diagnosed as LD if "the child fails to achieve a rate of learning to make sufficient progress to meet state-approved results in one or more of the areas identified in paragraph (a)(1) of this section when assessed with a response to scientific, research-based intervention process" (P.L. 108-446, § 300.309). Thus, NCLB and IDEA were inexorably and forever linked.

It is important to recognize the contextual basis for RTI in order to understand what it is and why we do it. The goal of RTI is not to identify children who are "truly LD" or even to improve the diagnostic procedures, but to enhance the learning of all children. The accountability movement led to an increased interest in monitoring how well children are learning; research on instruction for children with disabilities showed us that our instruction for these children matters and that they can learn; and research on special education suggested that changes were needed. The culmination of these events has led to a data-based decision-making model to enhance learning for all children.

WHAT IS IT?

RTI should perhaps be conceptualized much the same way that we view positive behavior supports (Sugai & Horner, 1999) because both involve the targeting of resources to student needs. Thus, RTI involves four components: (1) systematic use of assessment data; (2) efficient allocation of resources; (3) enhanced learning; and (4) applicability for all children. In other words, the goal is to seek instruction and intervention that will allow a child to be successful rather than identifying children for whom previous and presumed future interventions lacked success. Through this approach special education becomes the funding avenue for children whose needs are so intense that they require the resource expenditure allotted to special education.

The resource allocation model of RTI functionally places the primary jurisdiction over RTI in general education. Therefore, it is most effectively accomplished through a three-tiered model based on increasing intensity of service and frequency of assessment (Tilly, 2003), all of which is operated by general education. Table 1.1 is based on Burns, Deno, and Jimerson (2007) and lists the three tiers and the activities associated with each. Tier 1 of an RTI model involves quality core instruction in general education and benchmark assessments to screen students and monitor progress in learning. Students who do not make adequate progress in general education despite a sound core reading curriculum receive additional support in tier 2. Fuchs, Mock, Morgan, and Young (2003) characterize existing RTI models as either based on standard protocol or on problem solving. In other words, most RTI models have involved either a common intervention among all children who were not reading proficiently or interventions developed for individual students by problem-solving teams. However, Reschly (2003) has presented both of these approaches within one model, which seems

Table 1.1   The Three Tiers of RTI

Tier	% of Student Population	Description	Frequency of Assessment
1	All students	Universal: Adherence to a research-based core curriculum in general education.	Benchmark assessment at least three times/year.
2	Approximately 15%	Targeted: Small-group (three to five students) interventions delivered as part of general education.	At least monthly progress monitoring.
3	Approximately 5%	Intensive: Individualized interventions based on problem-solving models. Could include special education services.	At least weekly progress monitoring and frequent informal classroom-based assessments.

to make conceptual sense in that both seek to improve student learning and could probably work best within a unified model (Christ, Burns, & Ysseldyke, 2005). Thus, the critical component of tier 2 is to identify children who require remedial support and small-group interventions to accommodate the approximately 15% of the student population for whom tier 1 services are not sufficient. Moreover, student reading progress and fluency level are usually used to identify children as requiring more intensive interventions. Therefore, tier 2 interventions have a standardized component to assure efficiency and are delivered in small groups of four to six students.

Students who do not adequately respond to interventions provided in tiers 1 or 2 receive daily individualized interventions for at least 30 minutes per day with at least weekly progress monitoring in tier 3. These interventions are usually developed from a problem-analysis procedure often involving a problem-solving team and are delivered via general education. However, if the individualized interventions required for the child to be successful are extensively resource intensive, then special education resources would be committed to sustain success and the child would be identified as having a disability.

WHAT WOULD HAPPEN?

Implementing RTI on the national level would have widespread implications for children given that those diagnosed as LD represent over 50% of all children identified with a disability and approximately 5% of the total school population (Lerner, 2002). Therefore, some have prognosticated negative affects for children (Hale, Naglieri, Kaufman, & Kavale, 2004). We cannot accurately predict what will happen if RTI is implemented nationwide or in an individual school district, but we can examine what has happened when RTI is implemented in local schools or even on a statewide level.

Outcomes

A meta-analysis of research found that RTI led to improved systemic outcomes (e.g., reduction in children referred to and placed into special education programs) and student progress (e.g., higher achievement scores, reduced behavioral difficulties, etc.; Burns, Appleton, & Stehouwer, 2005). More specifically, it has been found that an incresed number of children demonstrate proficiency on state accountability tests (Heartland Area Education Agency 11, 2004; Sornson, Frost, & Burns, 2005), reading skills improved among children identified as at risk for reading failure (Marston, Muyskens, Lau, & Canter, 2003; Tilly, 2003), and children demonstrated increased time on task, task completion, and task comprehension during instruction (Kovaleski, Gickling, Morrow, & Swank, 1999).

Special education in RTI models becomes much more special in that children with disabilities receive greater services and additional specialized instruction than they do through more traditional approaches (Ikeda & Gustafson, 2002; Reschly & Starkweather, 1997). Moreover, these services begin at earlier grades (Reschly & Starkweather, 1997) because the dependency on a discrepancy between intelligence and achievement scores associated with traditional LD diagnostic approaches has made it almost impossible for many children to score low enough on a standardized norm-referenced achievement test in order to cause such a discrepancy to appear. Thus, a "wait to fail" model (Donovan & Cross, 2002) has been used in which the child is tested and retested until approximately grades 3 or 4, when a discrepancy can be detected; unfortunately, a critical window of learning has closed by then (Snow, Burns, & Griffin, 1998).

The *Twenty-Fourth Annual Report to Congress on the Implementation of the Individuals with Disabilities Education Act* (U.S. Department of Education, 2002) reports that 2,887,217 school-age children were identified with a learning disability, which equals 5.7% of the total estimated student population in this country. On average, less than 2% of the student population in various studies and program evaluations of RTI is identified as LD (Burns et al., 2005). Thus, concerns about large numbers of children identified as LD, or the "open the floodgates" concern about RTI (Hale et al., 2004) were not validated by previous research. However, approximately 6% of the student population in these studies is referred to the RTI model through problem-solving teams and the like (Burns et al., 2005), a number that closely matches the aforementioned national prevalence estimates for LD. Thus, the number of children experiencing difficulties is somewhat constant, but approximately 4% of the student population receives adequate support through a tiered intervention model and does not require an LD diagnosis.

Given that children's needs are better met in general education, and special education becomes more intense and individualized, special education services also become more efficient. Sornson et al. (2005) found that when an RTI approach is implemented in one school district, the percentage of children identified with a special education disability declines from 10.2% to 6.6% over a 10-year period, but the state average during that same time period increased from 10.8% to 13.4%. If this particular district had to keep up with the state average—in other words, if its prevalence rate grew at the same rate—it would have had to increase spending by $2.9 million. If its disability prevalence rate matched the national average of 11% of the student population, then it would have had to increase spending for special education by almost $2 million. Thus, children's needs are being met, but at an overall decreased cost.

The National Association of State Directors of Special Education is currently publishing a book that details the research base for RTI (Griffin, Parson, Burns, VanDerHeyden, 2007), which is quite extensive. That is, the research supporting the various components of RTI is well established, but it is somewhat limited when examining the compilation of those components into one model. We have learned much from our predecessor, but much remains to be learned.

QUESTIONS TO CONSIDER IN YOUR SCHOOL DISTRICT

The aforementioned meta-analysis of RTI research (Burns et al., 2005) had one interesting finding: that RTI initiatives that are field based (started by school district staff and existing before the research was conducted) led to better effectiveness than those started by university faculty for the purposes of research. Although there are several plausible explanations for these findings, one could be that the RTI implementation process is a long one that requires an extended period of training, refinement, and retraining. In other words, when RTI is implemented in a local school or district, unforeseen difficulties will occur that need to be addressed through a modified model and retraining. This is an especially critical point because implementation integrity of the RTI process may very well be the most significant obstacle to implementation on a national level. Several questions need to be addressed both at the national and local levels. Listed herein are a few of the more critical questions with which local school districts will need to struggle.

Leadership

Research on school effectiveness consistently finds that instructional leadership on the part of the school principal is a critical component (Levine & Lezotte, 1990). Thus, effective leadership is important for success in schools, and RTI is no exception—but who should lead the effort? Most districts center RTI implementation within special education departments and provide leadership through the director and supervisors of special education. Although special education should be involved, RTI should be perceived as a general education initiative with leadership coming from building principals, school superintendents and assistant superintendents, and other general education administrators such as curriculum directors. Perhaps districts could assemble a leadership team made up of various disciplines, including special education, but general education's leadership role needs to be explicit.

Training and Professional Development

Some have wondered if schools have sufficiently trained personnel to successful implement RTI (Vaughn & Fuchs, 2003). We believe that many practitioners have the basic skills necessary for RTI (e.g., assessment, data-based decision making, reading instruction, etc.), but that talent and expertise need to be pooled into one multidisciplinary resource. School psychologists may bring expertise in collecting and using data, but it may be the school's reading specialist who guides intervention selection efforts. However, all need some level of training in the basic RTI model and local specific implementation guidelines before implementation to assure common understanding, language, and goals. Discussing how this is best accomplished would exceed the scope of this book, but we can state that training efforts should include some measure of ongoing coaching (perhaps through study teams) and performance feedback in the basic components laid out in the present volume.

The Secondary Level

RTI implementation has clearly focused on elementary grades, with few attempting it on the secondary level. Some models do exist, as will be discussed later in this book, and have resulted in positive outcomes for students (Windram, Scierka, & Silberglitt, 2007). However, school districts will need to decide *when* and *how*—rather than *if*—RTI will begin in their middle schools and high schools. We suggest focusing on elementary schools in the initial phase of implementation, but eventually including secondary schools in practice and throughout the planning process.

The Parental Role

Most current RTI initiatives only involve parents in a perfunctory and superficial manner through obligatory methods such as parental notification (Lau et al., 2005). Given that longitudinal research has found positive and direct links between academic achievement and parental involvement (Englund, Luckner, Whaley, & Egeland, 2004), including parents in the RTI process in meaningful ways seems important. However, what that would entail is yet to be conclusively determined and should probably be addressed based on the unique needs of the district and its relationship with its parents. We suggest including parent representatives on planning committees and forming a separate group to suggest how to best engage parents in student learning within the RTI model.

THE PRESENT VOLUME

Although school districts across the country are implementing RTI approaches to better meet the needs of all children, current resources that discuss effective implementation are limited in availability and scope. This is important given that implementation integrity has repeatedly been identified as perhaps the most significant obstacle to large-scale implementation for RTI (Burns & Ysseldyke, 2005; Gansle & Noell, 2006; Ysseldyke, 2005). Thus, the goal of this book is to provide a resource for practitioners that will discuss how to implement RTI in easily understood terms and easily implemented procedures. Specifically, chapter 2 will discuss assessments to use at each grade level and how to structure data collection so that data can be quickly and efficiently conducted, as well as methods for progress monitoring and methods with which to store, access, and present data. Chapter 3 also addresses assessment, but will focus on how to use data for instructional and intervention decisions; thus, the chapter will discuss deriving benchmark and target goals, how to judge adequate progress toward goals in all three tiers, and how data can be used for special education eligibility decisions. Chapter 4 depicts how to organize the school, school personnel, and school day to best accomplish successful implementation, and chapter 5 discusses a scientifically based curriculum for all children and how to differentiate classwide versus individual difficulties. Chapters 6 and 7 address tiers 2 and 3, respectively, in that the former lays out how to best organize small groups for intervention (tier 2) and the latter focuses on detailed problem analysis to best identify specific interventions for individual children (tier 3). Finally, chapter 8 presents common difficulties in RTI implementation and suggestions for addressing them.

Our hope is that this book will assist the efforts of those actually doing the work. We provide several examples of forms and materials that can be used on the accompanying CD that can be used as is or modified to meet the unique strengths and needs of various schools and school districts. Our motivation for this book is that we have seen RTI improve the education of countless children and believe that it can help districts be more effective and efficient. However, we are concerned that schools will implement ineffective practices in the name of RTI, or will implement an effective model without fidelity, both of which will result in a lack of improved student outcomes and a continuation of the status quo. Thus, our fear is that RTI will be abandoned without ever truly being tested, as is so often the case with new methods in education. In fact, Ellis has stated that "today's flagship is tomorrow's abandoned shipwreck" (2001, p. 253) as a nod to how often schools try something new in the never-ending search for improvement, only to give up shortly thereafter because the "new" initiative was not based on research or was not implemented correctly; this is why we emphasize the importance of implementation integrity. RTI is not anything particularly new, but could result in improved outcomes if practitioners are adequately trained and supported and various implementation issues are considered before hand. We hope that the present volume will help with both.

2

Assessments within
an RTI System

A strong measurement system is the cornerstone of any successful response-to-intervention (RTI) process. Without assessment of student progress, educators will be unable to determine whether instruction and interventions are working to promote positive student outcomes. Successful implementation of an RTI model requires a measurement system that can accomplish two purposes: First, the system must be used to screen all students regularly for achievement difficulties; second, students who are identified as below target or at risk should have their academic progress monitored more frequently to assist teachers in determining whether additional intervention is successful.

The federal government's No Child Left Behind Act mandates that all students must be assessed by at least grade 3 (P.L. 107-110, 2001). While the goal to have students reading proficiently by grade 3 is admirable, schools cannot afford to wait that long to assess student reading and other basic skills. Educators must know from the earliest possible moment who is or is not succeeding and intervene accordingly. This chapter will discuss assessments to use at each grade level and how to structure data collection so that data can be quickly and efficiently conducted, as well as methods for progress monitoring and methods with which to store, access, and present the data. This chapter will primarily focus on the use of curriculum-based measurement (CBM) as a system to use for universal screening and progress monitoring. Kame'enui (2002) has deemed curriculum-based measures of reading (CBM-R) sufficient for use in screening progress monitoring.

TYPES OF ASSESSMENTS FOR RTI

Assessment data are either collected for summative or formative evaluations, both of which are important to the instructional process and lead to improved outcomes (Fuchs & Fuchs, 1986; Fuchs, Fuchs, Hamlett, & Allinder, 1991; Fuchs, Fuchs, Hosp, & Hamlett, 2003; Salvia, Ysseldyke, & Bolt, 2007). Summative evaluation is the collection of data after instruction occurs to make judgments about the instruction such as "grading, certification, evaluation of progress, or research on effectiveness" (Bloom, Hastings, & Madaus, 1971, p. 117). Thus, any assessment that examines what a child has learned or not learned from previous instruction could be conceptualized as part of a summative evaluation. Conversely, formative evaluation is the "systematic evaluation in the process of curriculum construction, teaching, and learning for the purposes of improving any of these three processes" (Bloom et al., 1971, p. 117). Thus, the essential attribute of formative evaluation is that the data are used to identify student needs and to plan instruction that will better meet those needs (William, 2006), which often involves assessing the knowledge of terms and facts, rules and principles for the tasks, processes and procedures necessary for successful completion, and the ability to translate or apply the information (Bloom et al., 1971). As can be seen from these succinct descriptions, activities in which practitioners engage vary substantially between formative and summative evaluations. Thus, the types of assessments used should also vary.

General Outcome Measures

General outcome measures (GOMs) are standardized measures that assess proficiency of global outcomes associated with an entire curriculum (Fuchs & Deno, 1991). Moreover, GOMs are assessments of general outcomes and are often used in progress monitoring, which involves keeping track of children's academic development in order to make changes to instruction based on progress or the lack thereof (Speece, n.d.). The most commonly used and well-researched GOM is CBM. The goal of GOMs is to assess instructional effectiveness and quickly make changes as needed. As such, they function as summative evaluations because these data are used to judge the effectiveness of instruction and may suggest a need for change, but the data do not suggest how to change. In fact, Bloom et al.'s definition specifically lists "evaluation of progress" (1971, p. 117) as an example of summative evaluation. Although GOM data become more formative in nature when they are used to establish goals, formative evaluation probably cannot rely entirely on data from GOMs. However, GOM data are ideally suited for monitoring progress toward a goal.

Subskill Mastery Measurement

The second category of assessments, subskill mastery measures (SMMs), are assessments of smaller domains of learning based on predetermined criteria for mastery (Fuchs & Deno, 1991). SMMs can be closely aligned with formative evaluation because they are used to directly assess the learning unit to identify student strengths and needs before instruction occurs. Curriculum-based assessment for instructional design (Gravois & Gickling, 2002) is the most well-researched SMM, with research supporting the reliability of the data and the validity of the resulting decisions (Burns, 2004a, 2004b; Burns, 2007; Burns et al., 2000).

The goal of SMM is usually to determine if the student has mastered the task and whether or not the individual task demands match the student's skill level. This is often accomplished by comparing scores to criteria for an instructional or independent level, such as 93–97% known words within a reading task for an instructional level and 98% or higher for an independent level (Gravois & Gickling, 2002) or, in mathematics, 14 to 31 digits correct per minute for grades 2 and 3 and 24 to 49 digits correct per minute for grades 4 and 5 (Burns, VanDerHeyden, & Jiban, 2006). The independent level for mathematics would simply be a score of digits correct per minute that exceeded the highest end of the instructional level range for the specified grade. Moreover, the assessment stimuli are much more focused than GOMs in that the probes for GOMs would represent the entire curriculum, and SMM only examines one aspect thereof (e.g., letter sounds, single-digit addition, etc.). Thus, SMMs are used to determine how much about a subject and what specifically in the subject the student already knows before instruction begins. These data are then used to plan instruction or to modify instruction as it progresses.

CURRICULUM-BASED MEASUREMENT

When you go to a doctor, she checks your height, weight, temperature, and blood pressure, among other things. Although these measures do not assess everything about your health, they can function as indicators to your doctor of problems that may exist. (For example, if your temperature is elevated, your doctor may order more tests to determine if you have an infection.) These indicators are simple, efficient, accurate, and inexpensive. Education has its own set of indicators in basic skills areas, often referred to as CBM or GOMs. CBM allows teachers to formatively evaluate their instruction for individual students on an ongoing basis (Deno, 1985; Deno, Marston, Shinn, & Tindal, 1983; Deno, Mirkin, & Chiang, 1982). Such frequent measurement prompts teachers to adjust instruction as needed to effect more progress for each student (Deno & Fuchs, 1987). Furthermore, evidence exists that when individual progress monitoring is used in a formative evaluation design, intervention effectiveness can be increased (Fuchs & Fuchs, 1986.). In addition, schools can use the same measure to regularly evaluate their overall instructional programs (Deno, 2003).

A considerable amount of research has been conducted (Good & Jefferson, 1998; Marston, 1989) that examines the technical adequacy of the measures indicating adequate reliability and validity. In addition, there is substantial evidence for the construct validity (Shinn, Good, Knutson, Tilly, & Collins, 1992) and criterion-related validity with other measures (Deno et al., 1982; Fuchs, Fuchs, & Maxwell, 1988). Data on over 5,000 students from the St. Croix River Education District (SCRED) in Minnesota indicate significant statistical correlations between CBM and a group reading test used as a state accountability measure that ranges from .51 to .71 (Silberglitt, Burns, Madyun, & Lail, 2006).

In addition to adequate psychometric properties, we advocate using CBMs to measure student response within an RTI system for a number of other reasons. First, the measures are simple, quick, and inexpensive. Because the measures are short fluency measures, they can be given to students in less than 5 minutes and result in minimal lost instructional time. Second, the measures are easily understood by both parents and teachers. Third, because the measures can be given often and are sensitive to growth over a short period of time, teachers can use the data to inform their instruction and evaluate intervention effects.

Kameenui and Simmons (1998) presented a schoolwide intervention model in which students were measured on three schedules using CBM: *benchmark*, for all students grades K–8 (three times per year); *strategic*, for students of some concern (once per month); and *intensive*, for students of great concern (once per week). Commonly used GOMs include *reading*

Table 2.1 A Summary of Commonly Used General
Outcome Measures

Area	Time	Procedure	Scoring (per minute)
Early literacy			
Letter naming	1 minute	Individual	Letter names correct
Letter sounds			Letter sounds correct
Phonemic segmentation			Segments correct
Nonsense-word			Letter sounds correct
Reading			
Oral reading fluency	1 minute	Individual	Words read correctly
Maze	3–5 minutes	Group or individual	Words correct
Math			
Computation	2–5 minutes	Group or individual	Correct problems
Concepts			Correct digits
Early numeracy			
Oral counting	1 minute	Individual	Correct oral counts
Missing number			Correct missing numbers
Number identification			Correct number identification
Quantity discrimination			Correct quantity discriminations
Written expression	3–5 minutes	Group or individual	Total words written Correct words sequence Words spelled correctly
Spelling	2 minutes	Group or individual	Correct words Correct letter sequence

Note: MAZE = Procedure in which every fifth word is omitted and the child selects from these options.

(i.e., oral reading fluency); *early literacy measures* (letter naming fluency, letter sound fluency, nonsense word fluency, and phonemic segmenting and blending tasks), *mathematics* (math fact fluency, and math concepts and applications), *early numeracy* (quantity array, quantity discrimination, and number identification), and *written expression* (correct word sequences). These measures are summarized in Table 2.1. Within a three-tier model, benchmark assessment is typically conducted at tier 2, strategic assessment at tier 2, and intensive assessment at tier 3. Although the time periods at which students are monitored differ, the administration and scoring procedures are the same. The next section will provide a detailed discussion of benchmark assessment procedures, along with tips for practitioners on how to organize and conduct benchmark assessment.

BENCHMARK ASSESSMENT

Benchmark assessment is conducted with all students three times per year in the fall, winter, and spring and serves a number of purposes. First, it is a screening tool that monitors the progress of every student, calling attention to any student who is having difficulty and might have escaped the attention of the school staff. This signals the need to monitor the student more often. Second, it establishes school norms that can be used to set goals. Third, benchmark data may be used to evaluate the effectiveness of the school's basic skills programs.

Prior to conducting benchmark assessment, we recommend conducting a short (i.e., 1 hour) training session with general education teachers. There are four purposes of this training session. First, the teachers need to be provided with a description of the measures to be used including a brief overview of administration and scoring procedures. Second, the technical adequacy of the measures should be reviewed so that teachers may have confidence in the data that is generated. Third, teachers need to understand how the measures are linked to instruction and intervention. Fourth, an overview of the different decisions that can be made with the measures should be provided. Without some type of general overview for all staff, the likelihood of resistance to data collection increases, and the teaching staff will not understand the utility of the measurement system.

The Logistics of Benchmark Assessment

Prior to conducting benchmark assessment, there are a number of decisions to be made, including identifying measures to use, determining who will conduct the assessment, and determining how to train the assessors. Once these decisions have been made, schools need to determine the actual procedures for data collection. Finally, after data have been collected, decisions need to be made about how to communicate results to teachers and parents and use the information to inform instruction. These different decisions are covered in more detail in the following sections.

Table 2.2   A Sample Timeline for Administering Early Literacy
Benchmark Assessments

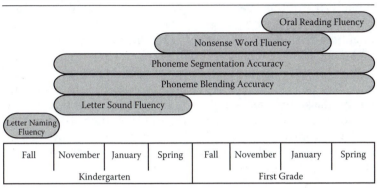

Fall	November	January	Spring	Fall	November	January	Spring
	Kindergarten				First Grade		

Identifying the Measures to Be Used

The first step in conducting benchmark assessment is to determine which measures will be used at each benchmark period. An array of GOMs exist in the areas of early literacy, early numeracy, reading, math, written expression, and spelling. Table 2.1 provides an example of the different measures used for grades K–8. Table 2.2 provides a sample timeline of when to administer early literacy and reading measures in kindergarten and grade 1.

Selecting an Assessment Window

We recommend that districts identify a standard time frame for collecting benchmark data. Using a standard assessment window will allow comparisons to be made across school years for program evaluation purposes. One common time frame used is to collect benchmark data for the fall season during the last two weeks of September, winter benchmark data during the last two weeks of January, and spring benchmark data during the last two weeks of May. Once particular dates have been selected, it is critical that all schools within the district collect data during the specified time frames.

Identifying a Measurement Team

Once the measures to be used have been identified, the next step is to identify a measurement team that will conduct the assessment. Benchmark assessment is conducted in the fall, winter, and spring by having a cadre of trained individuals test each student in every classroom. With 12 testers, a classroom of 24 students can be tested in 10–15 minutes (at approximately 5 minutes per child). While each school may have different members on its team, we have found that appropriate members include paraprofessionals, Title One teachers, special education teachers, school psychologists, and community volunteers. In addition, some schools that we work with use National Honor Society Students from high schools and paraprofessionals as testers. In some cases, classroom teachers conduct benchmark assessments of their own students, but our experience has shown that it is usually best to have a team conduct benchmark assessment to help assist with the teacher "buy-in" of the process.

Training the Measurement Team

Once the measurement team has been identified, it needs to be trained on administration and scoring of the measures. We suggest conducting a training session before each benchmark assessment. Training of the team members typically takes around 90 minutes. Initial training should include administration and scoring of the measure, how to record student scores, and issues around data privacy. Initial training should include practice and feedback on administering and scoring the measures, either by watching a videotape of a student reading aloud or by practicing with actual students.

Gathering Necessary Materials

We recommend administering three passages or probes to each student and using the median score as the representative score. Each examiner will need one set of student and examiner passages. We suggest that both sets of passages either be laminated or inserted in plastic overlays so that they can be reused. Each examiner will need a clipboard, a copy of the standardized administration instructions, a stopwatch or timer, dry-erase markers (two or three per person), and a damp sponge.

Identifying the Procedures for Data Collection

We suggest that a facilitator be named to coordinate the activities of the measurement team. Prior to collecting data, the team will need to determine the location at which the assessment will take place. The most efficient process is to have the team set up stations within the hallway outside the classrooms. After a grade level is completed, the team moves to the next location. Other possibilities include bringing the students to a central location such as the library, lunchroom, or other common area.

Once students arrive at the testing area, the following procedures are followed. First, students read three passages aloud to the examiners. The examiners score the student passages using dry-erase markers prior to reading with the next student. Examiners record the scores for each of the three passages along with the median of the three passages on the class list. At the end of the day, the examiners will give the facilitator their class lists for data entry. The facilitator can either make one master list to give to the person doing data entry or give that person all of the lists.

For group-administered assessments such as those for math, written expression, and maze, the classroom teacher can administer the measures to their group of students. Either the classroom teachers or another trained group of individuals can score the measures.

MANAGING, REPORTING, AND REVIEWING BENCHMARK DATA

Managing Benchmark Data

After the benchmark data have been collected, the scores need to be entered into a database. School districts will need to decide whether to create their own database and data management system using software such as Microsoft Excel or to purchase an Internet-based data management system such as Dynamic Indicators of Basic Early Literacy Skills (DIBELS) (www.dibels.uoregon.edu) or AIMSweb (www.edformation. com). Both of these software systems must be purchased by the school, and the rates vary according to each provider. In addition, each of these systems includes various reporting and analytic features.

Reporting Benchmark Data

A useful chart for an educational team planning instruction is a top-to-bottom listing of every student in the grade (see Figure 2.1). By comparing these data to the target or expected scores for that norm period, teachers see at a glance who is succeeding and who is not. Examining the entire grade level

Student Score Distribution by Service Classification
Hartford School District - Wilson Elementary
Grade 3: 2001–2002
Reading - Curriculum Based Measurement

Teacher ▲	Student ▲	Fall Corrects	Fall Errors	Fall SC	Winter Corrects	Winter Errors	Winter SC	Spring Corrects	Spring Errors	Service Code SC
	Targets	60			75			90		
Greehling	Twilley, L.	177		R	180		R	198		R
Greehling	Schall, S.	156		R	160		R	197		R
Greehling	Mclaughlin, U.	151		R	167		R	187		R
Rogers	Wilcoxen, K.	136		R	167		R	185		R
Greehling	Wilkins, J.	171		R	180		R	184		R
Jones	Jouett, F.	184		R	194		R	182		R
Johnson	Gnadinger, J.	145		R	144		R	179		R
Greehling	Ainsworth, O.	139		R	169		R	179		R
Greehling	Wilges, I.	107		R	172		R	178		R
Johnson	Gumm, D.	127		R	190		R	174		R
Johnson	Delong, B.	145		R	149		R	174		R
Greehling	Whitmire, R.	132		R	175		R	172		R

Teacher	Student	Fall Corrects	Fall SC	Winter Corrects	Winter SC	Spring Corrects	Spring SC
Greehling	Jenkins, D.	25	1	16	1	27	1
Johnson	Shewell, U.	65	S	20	R	24	S
Johnson	Sherrick, T.	12	S	13	S	21	S
Greehling	Hauso, I.	30	R	12	R	14	*

	Fall	Winter	Spring
Mean	84.4	102.4	113.9
Median	75.5	94.0	110.0
Number of Students Assessed	78	85	81

*Student is below target for the latest benchmark period.

R = Regular Ed   T = Title | S = Special Ed

Percentiles

90th	178.0	40th	96.0
75th	145.0	25th	85.0
50th	110.0	10th	60.0

Figure 2.1   A Sample Top-to-Bottom List of Students' Oral Reading Fluency Scores by Grade. AIMSweb © 2002 by Harcourt Assessment, Inc. With permission. All rights reserved.

of students allows teachers to determine how to most effectively use valuable yet scarce resources.

Figure 2.2 is an example of a report of benchmark scores used for program evaluation. It is a display of "box and whiskers" charts of every class in a school for each norm period. On the horizontal axis is listed each grade level and norming period (i.e., *2F* means second grade, fall), with words read correctly per minute shown on the vertical axis. Each box shows the middle 50% of the class, with the bottom of the box being the 25th percentile and the top of the box being the 75th percentile. A line within the rectangle marks the 50th percentile. The "whiskers" extend to the scores of the 90th and 10th percentiles. Target scores for each grade and norm period are shown as short heavy horizontal lines across each "box"—for example, second grade fall, winter, and spring target rates are 30, 55, and 80, respectively. The goal is to have 90% of the students in each class rise above the target. That is, when the entire box and bottom whisker are above the target, 90% of the students in a given class are achieving at the target level. This is far different from expecting the average (50th percentile) child to be at target and is in line with the idea of "leaving no child behind." Ninety percent of all students achieving the target rate seems an ambitious goal, but, as illustrated in Figure 2.2, the students and teachers are approaching the goal.

Another useful report is a chart showing the percentage of students at each grade level who met the target score for that benchmark period (see Figure 2.3). This is an excellent report for grade-level teams and schools to use to set their respective improvement goals. If large numbers of students are below target, this indicates a need to intervene at tier 1 and examine whether appropriate curriculum and instructional strategies are being used. Schools can also examine the percentage of students who are somewhat below target (tier 2) and well below target (tier 3) at each norm period.

Examining the charts from past years shows that while the targets for each grade at each norm period have stayed the same, the percent of students in each grade exceeding the target has gone up. For example, during school year 1997–98, only about 45% of the students in grade 3 during the winter measurement were at or above the target. By comparison, in school year 2001–2002, 75% of the students in grade 3 during winter measurement were at or above the target.

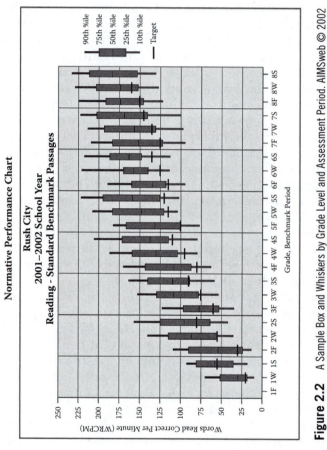

Figure 2.2 A Sample Box and Whiskers by Grade Level and Assessment Period. AIMSweb © 2002 by Harcourt Assessment, Inc. With permission. All rights reserved.

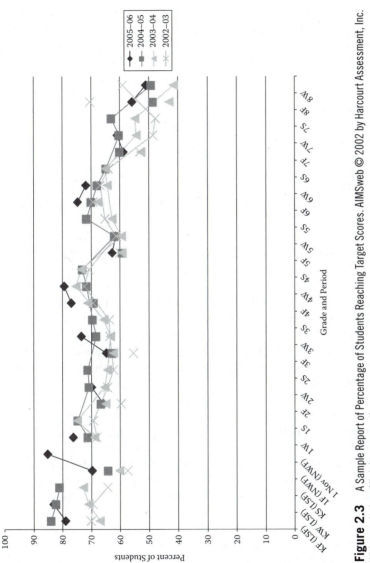

Figure 2.3   A Sample Report of Percentage of Students Reaching Target Scores. AIMSweb © 2002 by Harcourt Assessment, Inc. With permission. All rights reserved.

Using Benchmark Data within RTI: Determining Target Scores

After benchmark assessments are completed, the next step is to review data to determine which students are performing below expected levels or targets. To complete this task, districts must determine whether to use target scores or examine the distribution of students and identify students below a cut-off point (e.g., the 25th percentile) as at risk. When using target scores, two types of scores may be used: norm-referenced scores or criterion-referenced scores. Norm-referenced scores are used when a school district uses either school, district, state, or national normative scores. For example, an elementary school conducts benchmark assessment during the 2006–2007 school year. It decides to use the 50th percentile score at each benchmark period to determine target scores for each grade level for the 2007–2008 school year. This approach may be problematic if large numbers of students are experiencing academic difficulty. The target scores will be too low, and there is no incentive to raise the bar for all students. In these cases, it is suggested that schools use either state or national norms or a criterion-referenced approach.

In a criterion-referenced approach, target scores are set based on how well the target scores predict success on another measure—typically a high-stakes assessment. With the advent of the No Child Left Behind Act (2001) and high-stakes assessments, a criterion for success has been established in every state in the form of a specific score on the annual statewide assessment. This criterion is generally summative in nature and is not first measured until grade 3. General outcome measurement allows practitioners the flexibility to continue to measure formatively within and across school years, to begin measurement in early childhood and/or kindergarten, and to establish criteria for success along the way that will accurately predict whether a child is likely to also be successful on the statewide assessment. In addition, as statewide assessments change, or as concerns in their utility are raised, GOMs such as CBM will provide a trustworthy and proven alternative for effective data-driven decision making.

In the meantime, scores on CBM assessments can be linked to scores on statewide assessments such that a criterion for success is established at each grade level and time point of systemwide CBM assessment. For instance, a target score for CBM-R assessment for the spring season of grade 1 can be set such that students who reach that score are considered highly likely to be successful on the statewide assessment of reading in grade 3. Logistic regression allows the practitioner to create these target scores relatively simply and flexibly (Gibbons & Silberglitt, in press).

Logistic regression (LR) is a regression analysis procedure used when the dependent variable is categorical. Categorical variables consist of values that represent group membership (i.e., gender), while quantitative variables represent values where the numbers have meaning (i.e., test scores). In this case, the dependent variable is whether or not the student reaches grade-level standards on the upcoming statewide assessment, a categorical variable with two groups. Either quantitative or categorical independent variables are used to determine probabilities of membership in each of the categories of the dependent variable, using maximum likelihood estimation (Neter, Kutner, Nachtsheim, & Wasserman, 1996). In this case, LR calculates the probability (0–100%) that students will successfully reach grade-level standard based on their current CBM scores.

LR can be conducted at the local level by gathering data on students who have taken both the statewide assessment and the CBM assessment. To conduct the LR analysis, run the procedure in a statistical software program (such as SPSS), using CBM as the independent variable and whether or not students have reached grade-level standard on the state test as the dependent variable. The software program will generate values of β_0 and β_1, which can be put into the following formula, to determine the probability of reaching grade-level standard (written below as p) for a student with a given CBM score (written below as X):

$$p = (\exp(\beta_0 + \beta_1 X))/(1 + \exp(\beta_0 + \beta_1 X))$$

In addition, this formula can be graphed to provide a logistic response function, which is the curve of probabilities across the range of CBM scores. Figure 2.4 provides an example of such a curve, based on data from the St. Croix Education District, using CBM-R in the spring season of grade 3 to predict success on the statewide assessment. This same procedure can be used for GOMs given in earlier grades as well, providing formative criteria to predict success. (A Microsoft Excel document that produces these curves, based on values of β_0 and β_1 generated as described above, is available at the following web

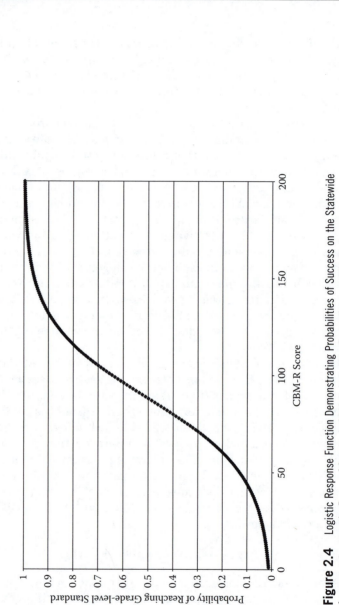

Figure 2.4 Logistic Response Function Demonstrating Probabilities of Success on the Statewide Assessment across the Range of Scores on CBM-R during the Spring Season of Grade 3.

Table 2.3   St. Croix River Education District
Target Scores in the Area of Reading

Grade	Fall	Winter	Spring	Growth Rate/Week
1	N/A	20	49	1.36
2	43	72	90	1.31
3	70	91	107	1.03
4	83	101	113	.83
5	108	128	136	.78
6	122	139	153	.86
7	137	148	158	
8	150	160	160	

address: http://www.scred.k12.mn.us/Research%20and%20 Outcomes/datalinks.htm.)

It is hoped that, in the future, CBM-oriented data ware-house services (e.g., AIMSweb, DIBELS, & EdCheckup) will provide both the calculation of the beta values and the logistic response function, thus providing practitioners with this goal-setting capability more efficiently, without the need for statistical software. In addition, these services could provide probability curves at both the local and state levels. A set of criterion-referenced benchmark scores from the St. Croix River Education District (SCRED) is included in Table 2.3. These scores are based on logistical regression procedures between general outcome measures of reading and the Minnesota State Accountability Tests.

Reviewing Benchmark Data

The last step in the benchmark assessment process is to review the data and use it to assist in decision making. Districts will need to determine who will take primary responsibility for reviewing benchmark data and how the information will be shared with grade-level teachers. For example, in some schools, the principal reviews benchmark data after each benchmark period and then meets with grade-level teams to review the data. In other schools, the problem-solving team may review the data. In the SCRED, a reading "coach" is assigned to every school. One of the roles of the coach is to meet with grade-level teams of teachers after every benchmark period. The teams review the data and use it to assist in making decisions about instructional groupings across the grade level. The teams also use the data to assist in grade-level goal setting. For example, if a third grade team of teachers met in the fall to review benchmark data and only 52% of students were at or above the target score at that time, they would then set a goal to increase the percentage of students at or above target at the winter and spring benchmark periods.

Although schoolwide benchmark data are useful for program evaluation and verifying the progress for students at or above goal, the real power of data collection comes when we monitor an individual student who is below goal level and use the data to inform his instruction. More frequent progress monitoring is referred to as either strategic or intensive monitoring and will be described in more detail in the next section.

STRATEGIC AND INTENSIVE MONITORING

After benchmark assessments are completed, the data must be reviewed to determine which students are performing below expected levels or targets. Subsequently, these students have their progress monitored either monthly (strategic monitoring) or weekly (intensive monitoring). Strategic and intensive monitoring serve four purposes. First, each student has an individual graph displaying his data in relation to his goal. This graph provides a basis for evaluating instructional programming for individual students as the instruction is occurring. The data are used to guide instructional decisions. Second, the graph helps the educational team make ongoing decisions about goals, materials, levels, and groups. Once regular data are collected and examined by teachers, there is a natural inclination to want to find more effective ways to raise achievement for all students. This leads the teachers to a search for more powerful instructional techniques. Third, graphically displayed data aid communication with parents and other professionals. Many schools that we work with provide a copy of student graphs to parents during parent-teacher conferences. Parents have reported that they appreciate being able to see how their child performs relative to other students in their child's grade. Finally, the information on the graph can be used to document progress for individual education plan (IEP) students as required by law for periodic and annual reviews.

The Logistics of Strategic and Intensive Measurement
Identifying Who Will Collect Data
Progress monitoring data may be collected by a variety of school staff including reading teachers, regular education

teachers, special education teachers, paraprofessionals, and volunteers. In the SCRED, paraprofessionals often collect these progress monitoring data, whereas the teachers are responsible for examining the data often and using it to make instructional decisions. In many cases, paraprofessionals may collect the majority of the progress monitoring data, but the teacher providing instruction may also collect data intermittently. While there is not a hard and fast rule, we have found that the most efficient way to collect data is to have a schedule developed with the names of all students in a grade level to be progress monitored, record the dates (or days of the week) of monitoring, and identify the person responsible for conducting the monitoring.

Identifying How Often Data Will Be Collected

In the area of reading, progress monitoring data typically are collected either monthly or biweekly for students at tier 2 and either weekly or twice weekly for students at tier 3. The general rule is that the more discrepant the student is from the target score, the more frequent her progress should be monitored. In the areas of math and writing, assessment more than twice per month on math applications and written expression measures is not recommended due to the insensitivity of the measures. Often the frequency of data collection is dependent on resources available to conduct monitoring.

Identifying Measurement Material

We recommend monitoring students out of grade-level passages whenever possible. At tier 3, there will be instances where students will be monitored using passages below their current grade level. For students on IEPs this decision will be made by the IEP team. Gibbons and Howe (1999) reported a lower standard error of measurement and greater sensitivity when monitoring students who were severely discrepant from grade-level expectations (i.e., reading 2 or more years below grade level) using materials one grade level above their *instructional level*. For example, consider Susie, a fifth grader reading 13 words correctly per minute in the fall. The target score for fifth grade is 120 words correctly per minute. When Susie is given reading passages in consecutively lower grade-level materials (i.e., survey-level assessment), we find that her instructional level corresponds to the spring of grade 3. In this case, the team may decide to monitor Susie out of grade 3 material rather than grade 5. More information about assessing an instructional level is presented in chapter 3.

REPORTING AND REVIEWING PROGRESS MONITORING DATA

Reporting Progress Monitoring Data

All students receiving strategic or intensive monitoring should have an individual graph that displays their data. Each graph should have an "aim line" in which to compare student data. The aim line is drawn by connecting the median baseline data point to the final goal. Schools will need to determine whether to use an electronic graphing system or paper graphs. Both DIBELS and AIMSweb have features that will graphically display data. An example of a graph created by AIMSweb is displayed in Figure 2.5. Graphs also may be created using Microsoft Excel, although this process is a bit more labor intensive than using an Internet-based system or a paper graph. An example of a graph created by Microsoft Excel is displayed in Figure 2.6. Finally, student data points may be recorded on paper graphs. If this option is selected, we recommend that districts design a graph that will span the entire school year. Once the graph is designed, we recommend having it printed on card stock. An example of a paper graph is displayed in Figure 2.7.

Regardless of the type of graph chosen, a system needs to be established for recording data on the graph. Some schools we have worked with have one person in charge of entering data on the computer program or on the paper graph. In other instances, each person who collects progress monitoring data records the data on the student's graph. We recommend that the school measurement team meet annually to make these decisions and to review and troubleshoot any issues.

Reviewing Progress Monitoring Data

Once progress monitoring data are collected, the data must be used to aid in instructional decision making. Thus, schools will need to determine the process for reviewing student data. We recommend setting up a regular data review meeting. In the SCRED, grade-level teams meet weekly to review student data. These teams consist of all teachers within the grade level, along with specialists (e.g., reading teachers, Title One teachers, school psychologists, etc.). The teams meet in

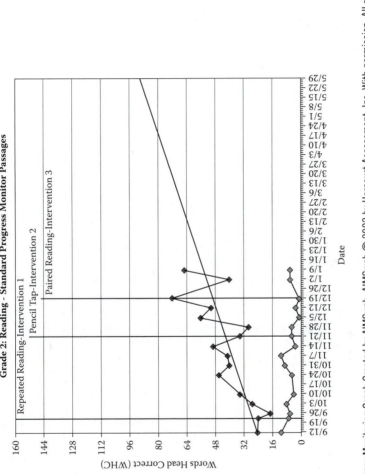

Figure 2.5 in the graph area:

Grade 2: Reading - Standard Progress Monitor Passages

Repeated Reading-Intervention 1

Pencil Tap-Intervention 2

Paired Reading-Intervention 3

Words Head Correct (WHC)

Date

Figure 2.5 A Sample Progress Monitoring Graph Created by AIMSweb. AIMSweb © 2002 by Harcourt Assessment, Inc. With permission. All rights reserved.

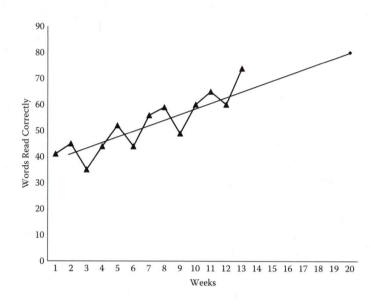

Figure 2.6 A Sample Progress Monitoring Graph Created by Microsoft Excel.

a classroom and use a projector to view electronic copies of student graphs. The teams review all students who are below target and discuss the students' rate of progress toward their goals. If progress is insufficient, the team discusses whether to change the instructional program. Other schools may have a data team that meets weekly to review student graphs. Following the meeting, a representative from the team follows up and consults with teachers of students who are not making adequate progress.

If schools opt to use paper graphs, we recommend that the graphs be maintained in binders in each teacher's classroom. While it is a bit cumbersome for the data recorder to go to each classroom to record data on the graph, we have found that teachers are much more likely to look at graphs if they are accessible in their classrooms. Finally, if a paper graph system is used, then copies of the individual graphs need to be made prior to each data review meeting.

CONCLUSION

RTI is the systematic use of data to enhance the learning of all students (Burns & VanDerHeyden, 2006). Without screening and progress monitoring data, schools will not accurately identify students at risk for academic failure and, more

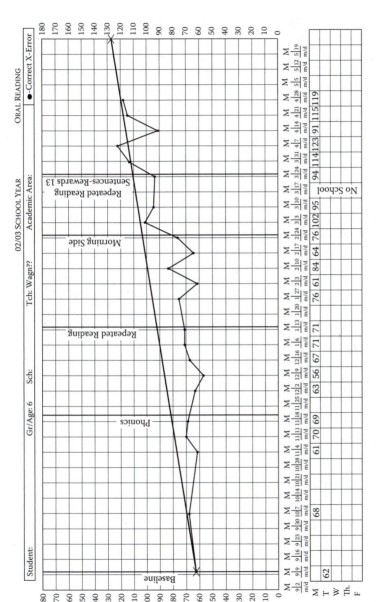

Figure 2.7 A Sample Paper Graph.

important, will not be able to determine if the interventions provided to students are effective. This is an era in which schools are becoming increasingly accountable for student outcomes. This accountability movement clearly *necessitates* the use of student outcome data to evaluate the effectiveness of the instruction provided to all students. The educational research literature contains numerous references to results, but results have rarely become operationalized. Using valid and reliable student outcome data is one way to operationalize educational results.

3

Data-Based Decision Making

During a recent workshop about response-to-intervention (RTI), one person asked, "I'm a classroom teacher; how will my life be different?" The answer involved a few points, but the first and primary one was that assessment data will actually be used to make decisions about instruction, interventions, and entitlement. Assessment is the key to RTI and to effective instruction in general, but even the most reliable and valid assessment system is meaningless until the data are interpreted and used. Much as how the purpose of the assessment drives the types of data collected, it also drives the types of decisions made and the criteria by which they are made.

As shown in Figure 3.1, as children's needs dictate a progression through the three tiers, three things also occur. First, measurement becomes more frequent: assessments in tier 1 are conducted three times a year, but they may be conducted daily or at least once or twice weekly in tier 3. Second, measurement becomes more precise: in tier 1, only general outcome measures such as oral reading fluency are used, but within tiers 2 and 3, data collection may involve much more specific subskill measures such as mastery of specific letter and/or phoneme sounds. Third, problem analysis becomes more detailed. As shown in Table 3.1, the problem-analysis foci change throughout the tiers and move from primarily problem identification to low-level analysis (e.g., classwide versus individual problems in tier 1, or identifying a category of problem in tier 2) to in-depth analysis in order to identify the specific cause of the problem. However, all tiers involve developing, implementing, and evaluating a plan (this is further discussed in chapter 7). This chapter will discuss problem-solving decisions made in each tier and the various decision-making rules used in each tier.

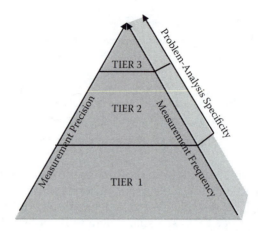

Figure 3.1   Relationships among Measurement, Problem-Solving Intensity, and the Three Tiers of RTI.

Table 3.1   Problem-Solving Foci in the Three Tiers

		Relevant Assessment	
	Problem-Solving Foci	**Data**	**Criteria**
Tier 1	Compare the skill level of the class to desired outcomes (problem identification).	GOM (e.g., oral reading fluency; ORF).	Comparison to national norms or empirically derived criteria.
Tier 2	Identify individual students who are discrepant from desired outcomes (problem identification). Identify category of difficulty (e.g., phonics versus fluency; problem analysis).	GOM (e.g., ORF) and SMM (e.g., nonsense-word fluency, phoneme segmentation fluency).	Normative comparison (e.g., lowest quartile) for GOM and fluency criteria for SMM. Dual discrepancy.
Tier 3	Identify functional cause of difficulty (problem analysis).	GOM and SMM.	Monitor progress with aimlineaim line and three-point comparisons, assess skills with mastery criteria. Dual discrepancy.

Notes: GOM = general outcome measures; ORF = oral reading fluency; SMM = subskill mastery measures

PROBLEM ANALYSIS DECISIONS AND DECISION-MAKING RULES

Tier 1

The Classwide Problem

A sound core curriculum is the foundation of RTI, and data should be gathered to assess if sufficient student learning is occurring. Moreover, research has consistently demonstrated that the first step in identifying individual students with significant difficulties is to rule out or factor out the effect of a classwide problem (VanDerHeyden & Burns, 2005; VanDerHeyden, Witt, & Naquin, 2003). This approach involves comparing the class median for the benchmark scores to a criterion, and those scores that fall below the criterion would be identified as a classwide problem; the intervention would thus focus on the class as a whole rather than on individuals. For example, VanDerHeyden and Burns (2005) have found classwide problems in mathematics and implemented a peer tutoring model within the classroom for approximately 15 minutes each day. After a few weeks, the class median increased until it exceeded the criterion, and the classwide problem was factored out. At that point individual students could then be targeted for additional intervention.

A median score, rather than an average, is used to determine a classwide problem because a classroom of students may range in size from 15 or 20 to as many as 35 or even 40. Smaller class sizes of less than 30 present a statistical problem because an average score would be too significantly affected by extreme scores, but median is not as adversely affected. For example, in a school where oral reading fluency (ORF) is assessed three times each year, data for individual students in each class would be reported to the teacher, but the median ORF score for that class would also be reported. Most database or data management systems easily compute the median for each class.

After identifying the class median, the score can then be compared to some criterion other than a local norm. Three options to which data can be compared are national norms, instructional-level criteria, and empirically derived criteria. (National norms for ORF are available at http://www.readnaturally.com/howto/whoNeeds.htm.) We suggest using the 25th percentile as the criterion because it represents the lowest end of the statistically average range. Thus, a third-grade classroom whose class median fell below the fall season criterion of 44 words

read correctly per minute would be deemed a classwide problem. Instructional-level criteria may also work for this purpose.
Gravois and Gickling's (2002) criteria of 93–97% known words
is well researched, but has not been used for this purpose. Deno
and Mirkin's (1977) criteria of 40–60 words (for grades 1 and 2)
and 70–100 words (grades 3–6) read correctly per minute have
been used to identify classwide problems, but those criteria
were derived from experience in one school in Minnesota (S.
L. Deno, personal communication, April 15, 2005), which suggests limited utility in other school districts across the country.
Thus, using the instructional level as a criterion is somewhat
problematic—with the possible exception of mathematics,
which has criteria that were derived through research (Burns,
VanDerHeyden, & Jiban, 2006).

The easiest option for classwide problem identification is
probably using a national norm, but there are better and more
complex options. For example, a school district could use its
own data and correlate those scores with state accountability
test scores and build a regression formula from the results. The
formula presented in chapter 2 could then be used to determine
what fluency score at each benchmark predicts a passing score
on the test. Alternatively, a district could conduct a receiver
operating characteristics curve analysis to determine which
score predicts a passing score on the state test. The resulting
criteria would have the advantage of being local and directly
linked to accountability tests, but should be validated through
estimates of sensitivity and specificity. Both of these options
are relatively simple and easily implemented if the school district has personnel trained in statistical methodologies (e.g., a
research and evaluation department or director); if not, then
the district may wish to use the national norm option.

Tier 2
Identifying Individual Students
After ruling or factoring out tier 1 problems, individual students can then be identified for additional intervention in
tier 2. Given that RTI is a resource allocation model, it is appropriate to target a percentage of the student population. In other
words, all individual students who score below the criterion
used to rule out the classwide problem could then be identified as needing additional intervention. However, it could be
possible that none or very few of the students would meet that

criterion. In this situation, the school would target the lowest 20% on the benchmark score in each grade.

As stated earlier, teachers would get benchmark scores for every student in their class and the class median. In addition, they would also receive the grade-level average score. If there are at least 35 students in the grade level, which is usually the case if there are multiple classrooms for each grade, then it is appropriate to use an average. These data would then be used to identify the 20th percentile, and all children who scored at or below the 20th percentile would be identified as needing a tier 2 intervention. If more than one score is used at the benchmark (e.g., letter-sound fluency and letter-naming fluency in kindergarten), then students at or below the 25th percentile for each score would be identified, and those who fell into that category on both scores would be targeted first. If there were three scores, then those that fell below the 25th percentile on all three would be targeted first, and those within that lowest quartile on two scores would be added until 20% of the student population was reached (e.g., two classrooms of second graders with 25 in each one would result in 10 students being identified for tier 2).

Category of Deficit

Remembering that tier 1 involves 80% of the student population and tier 2 involves 15–20%, the number of children served in these first two tiers is quite large. If there are 500 students in an elementary school, the result could be 100 students in tier 2, which is far too many to be able to conduct the level of problem analysis that will be discussed in chapters 4 and 7. Thus, the focus of problem solving in tier 2 is problem identification, with some low-level problem analysis to identify categories of deficits.

Once a student is identified as discrepant in the benchmark general outcome measures (GOMs), we then place him into a small-group intervention for tier 2. However, such an intervention is more effective if it correctly targets the skill deficit (Burns, VanDerHeyden, & Boice, in press). In reading, the work of the National Reading Panel (NRP, 2000) serves as the basis for this low-level analysis. The NRP reported four areas necessary for reading instruction—phonemic awareness, phonics, reading fluency, and vocabulary/comprehension—that could serve as the basis for small groups in that a school district could have a small-group intervention that focuses on phonics, one that focuses on reading fluency, and so on. (For more on this, see chapter 6.) Hence, after the GOMs identify a child as needing tier 2, more specific subskill mastery measures (SMMs) tools would be used to identify the specific skill deficit and resulting intervention.

Reading fluency is pretty straightforward because most school districts use ORF as the benchmark score in grades 2–6. Phonic skills could be assessed by administering a letter-sound or letter-word name fluency assessment for children in early elementary school, and nonsense-word fluency could be used for somewhat older children. These scores could then be compared to standards associated with Dynamic Indicators of Basic Early Literacy Skills (DIBELS; available online at http://dibels. uoregon.edu/benchmarkgoals.pdf). Teachers frequently report concerns about using skill measures such as letter-naming or nonsense-word fluency as measures of reading because neither represent authentic reading. In our opinion, those teachers are exactly *correct*, which is why these tools have limited utility as GOMs. However, both serve as a potential SMM that can be used to assess how well a student can sound out words in order to plan for instruction. Phonemic awareness can also be assessed fairly simply with phoneme segmentation fluency and also compared to DIBELS standards.

The code-based aspects of reading (phonemic awareness, phonics, and reading fluency) are easily measured, but reading comprehension is more complex. Research is currently underway at the University of Minnesota's Research Institute on Progress Monitoring to determine better methods of reading comprehension assessment for RTI, but as of today the maze procedure probably represents the best quick and dynamic assessment of reading comprehension (Shin, Deno, & Espin, 2000). (Interpretative criteria for maze are available for free from the Florida Center for Reading Research at http://www. fcrr.org/forf_mazes/mazes.htm.)

Adequate Progress

Student progress in tier 2 is typically assessed in terms of level and rate of achievement. Thus, interventions in tier 2 are deemed unsuccessful if the student's postintervention reading score is below a level of proficiency and growth is below a predetermined acceptable rate, both of which are determined with curriculum-based measurement (CBM). Data should ideally be collected at least weekly and no less than every other

Table 3.2   Computing Slope Estimates with Microsoft Excel

1. Open a new spreadsheet.

2. Label column A of row 1 *Student ID*, then columns B, C, D, etc., for as many sets of data that were collected (e.g., column B = September 2007; column C = January 2008; column D = May 2008).

A	B	C	D	E	F	G	H
Student ID	Sep-07	Jan-08	May-08				

3. Enter the score for each student in the corresponding column.

A	B	C	D	E	F	G	H
Student ID	Sep-07	Jan-08	May 08				
1	34	44	58				

4. Skip a column and enter the number of the week that the data were collected in the corresponding column. For example, if data were collected at the times listed in step 2 (above), then the weeks entered would be 2 (for September, assuming data were collected in the second week of the school year), 18 (for January, which is 16 weeks later), and 34 (for May, which is again 16 weeks later).

A	B	C	D	E	F	G	H
Student ID	Sep-07	Jan-08	May-08				
1	34	44	58		2	18	34

5. Highlight the three cells with the number of weeks (e.g., row 2, columns F, G, and H) and drag the cells into the rows for each student.

A	B	C	D	E	F	G	H
Student ID	Sep-07	Jan-08	May-08				
1	34	44	58		2	18	34
2	44	90	99		2	18	34
3	22	34	45		2	18	34

6. Place the cursor into row 2 (student 1) and column E, then click the function wizard *fx* and select slope. The *Y* variables (entered in the top space) are the CBM scores, which would be listed as B2:D2, and the *X* variables (entered in the bottom space) are the weeks, or F2:H2.

7. The resulting score is the slope estimate for those data. Highlight the cell containing the slope (cell E2) and drag it into the cells for all of the students.

A	B	C	D	E	F	G	H
Student ID	Sep-07	Jan-08	May-08	Slope			
1	34	44	58	0.75	2	18	34
2	44	90	99	1.71875	2	18	34
3	22	34	45	0.71875	2	18	34

Note: CBM = curriculum-based measurement.

week. Those data are then used to compute a slope of growth. Table 3.2 lists the steps for computing slopes from CBM scores in Microsoft Excel with the ordinary least squares method.

Discrepancies in level are defined by performances below benchmark standards (e.g., 40 words read correctly per minute in the spring season of grade 1) on postintervention CBM scores. Rate of growth is judged by computing slopes for each student and determining the average and standard deviation of the slope for each grade. Slopes that are more than one standard deviation below the grade average are considered discrepant. Thus, scores that result in a fluency level that is below a criterion and a slope that is more than one standard deviation below the average are considered dually discrepant (DD), and the intervention is considered unsuccessful.

Previous research has found that the DD approach is superior to a single discrepancy approach, which would rely on either a discrepancy in level or a discrepancy in the rate of achievement (L. S. Fuchs, 2003). Moreover, using a DD approach significantly differentiates scores on norm-referenced reading tests among children identified as at risk for reading failure (Burns & Senesac, 2005). Alternatively, the St. Croix River Education District in Minnesota uses a local norm-referenced approach for fluency (below the 7th percentile), but computes a criterion for slope (Silberglitt & Gibbons, 2005). Rates of growth are evaluated by correlating scores at the three benchmarks with state accountability data and deriving target scores that can be used to compute a target slope. For example, in third grade the fall target is 72, while the spring target is 107. Thirty-four weeks elapse between fall and spring benchmark testing, so the weekly growth rate of the targets is 1.03. This growth rate represents a criterion of a year's growth in a year's time (Silberglitt & Gibbons, 2005). Finally, a confidence interval around this criterion is computed, and students below this confidence interval are considered significantly below criterion (to assist in eligibility decisions), and students above the confidence interval are considered significantly above criterion (to assist in decisions about removing students from special education services). Thus, interventions that resulted in a postintervention level that fell below the 7th percentile and a slope of learning that fell below the confidence interval around the criterion for the grade level were considered unsuccessful (Silberglitt & Gibbons, 2005). Again, this approach appears to be quite promising (Burns, Silberglitt, Christ, & Gibbons, 2007), but more sophisticated statistical analysis skills are required.

Tier 3

As stated earlier, assessment in tier 3 is frequent and precise because in-depth problem analysis is needed to identify the cause of a problem. Thus, assessment in tier 3 is used to identify specific deficits, monitor progress toward goals, and make entitlement decisions such as providing special education services.

Identifying Specific Deficits

In order to identify specific deficits, two heuristics are used. First, the review, interview, observe and test approach and the instructional, curricular, environmental, and learner approach are used to generate hypotheses about problems and subsequent solutions; these are explained in some detail in chapter 7. However, the instructional hierarchy (Haring & Eaton, 1978) further delineates a student's skill functioning and can thus be used to target interventions (Burns et al., in press) and as a framework for problem analysis (Christ, in press).

Put this book down; put your hands together as if you were gripping a golf club, and then continue reading. You probably did one of four things: (1) you ignored this command because you have no idea how a golf club is held and do not care to know; (2) you remembered back to some previous time or something you observed and slowly clasped your hands in the interlocked grip, but may have interlocked the wrong fingers; (3) you recalled with little effort and somewhat easily created the golf grip; or (4) you created the proper golf grip in an almost automatic manner—that is, without even thinking about it. As humans learn new skills they follow a consistent pattern of phases that includes *acquisition, proficiency, generalization*, and *adaptation* (Haring & Eaton, 1978). When a student first learns something she is in the *acquisition* phase and is highly inaccurate and dysfluent; this would be the reader in our example who either did not even attempt the golf grip or really had to remember back to some other time and place to generate a grip that was probably incorrect. In the next phase of our example, one would be able to recall the golf grip with some effort and probably create it correctly; this is functioning within the *proficiency* phase, in which the skill can be performed with some effort, but requires time to do so (dysfluent). The last two stages involve the ability to use the newly acquired information in a different setting (*generalization*: learning the golf grip with a nine iron, but then using it with a five wood) and to solve novel problems (*adaptation*: using the golf grip to hold a child's baseball bat that is too small for one's hands to hold). Identifying in which stage a child is functioning can directly lead to interventions; this will be discussed elsewhere.

Most academic deficits involve the first two stages, *acquisition* and *proficiency*, and this is where assessment should start. Thus, the accuracy and proficiency (fluency) with which skills are completed are important data. Accuracy can be assessed by examining samples of student performance on particular problematic tasks (e.g., mathematics and writing) in order to determine if the student has acquired the basic skill, and timed assessments are required to determine the fluency of the skill in order to suggest the level of proficiency. For reading tasks, the accuracy criterion for the instructional level is especially useful. For example, if a second grader is reading 22 words correctly per minute in the spring, he is clearly dysfluent and lacking proficiency; however, we do not know if a fluency intervention is needed until we assess the accuracy. A child who is reading 85% of the words correctly is within the acquisition phase of learning for reading fluency and would require an accuracy intervention. However, if that same child was reading at the level of 94% known words, which falls within the 93–97% criterion, then a proficiency intervention would be needed.

The comparison of accuracy to proficiency mentioned above also applies to other areas presented by the NRP, with one exception. The accuracy criterion for the instruction level for any task other than reading for comprehension (e.g., math facts, learning sight words, practicing letter sounds, spelling, etc.) is less clear. A recent meta-analysis has found large effects for several accuracy percentages for these types of tasks, but the largest median effect was for 90% known words (Burns, 2004). Thus, 90% is probably the most appropriate accuracy criterion for these tasks. So, for example, if a first grader correctly names 15 letters in 1 minute at the end of the school year, she would be demonstrating a lack of proficiency, but if she correctly names 91% of them she would require additional practice, and if she named 75% of them she would need additional instruction in the sounds.

Monitoring Student Progress

Tier 3 becomes a systematic search for an effective intervention, of which progress monitoring is an important aspect. CBM data are collected at least once per week—though preferably twice each week—and are graphed. Afterward, an "aim line" is drawn to connect baseline functioning to target functioning in order to create a line of expected progress. Three consecutive data points below the aim line, as displayed in the top example of Figure 3.2, suggest that the intervention is not successful. A graph with data points that closely approximate the aim line, as shown in the bottom graph of Figure 3.2, suggests that the student is making adequate progress toward

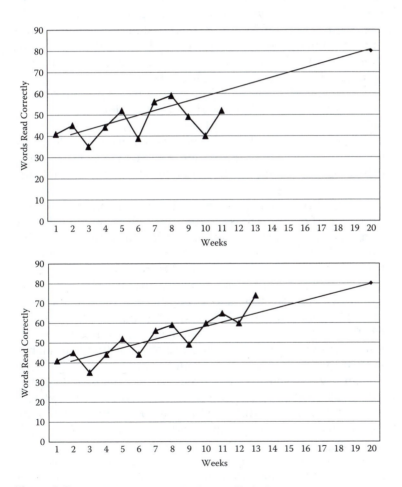

Figure 3.2   Sample Aim Line Graphs for Progress Monitoring.

achieving the goal. (Readers are referred to Shinn [1989] or websites such as www.studentprogress.org or www.progress-monitoring.org for detailed instructions on drawing an aim line.)

Determining Special Education Eligibility

The 2004 Individuals with Disabilities Education Act requires "a full and individual initial evaluation" prior to providing special education services (P.L. 108-466 § 614 [a][1][A]). Moreover, children with suspected disabilities must be assessed "in all areas related to the suspected disability" (§ 614 [b][3] [B]). Thus, the right to a comprehensive evaluation is again protected in special education law; but what is meant by the word *comprehensive*? It hardly seems possible that conducting one measure of intelligence and standardized measures of achievement could be more comprehensive than collecting data directly related to the problem for a period of weeks to measure the success of attempted interventions. Thus, a comprehensive evaluation could include screening child characteristics that might affect achievement (vision, hearing, etc.) along with direct assessment of current skills, instructional environments, and behaviors. In instances where the RTI data do not provide all the information needed for eligibility determination and classification, then additional relevant data are collected as needed.

Eligibility decisions within RTI result from students not making sufficient progress in tier 3 as judged by the presence of a dual discrepancy. In other words, if a student's reading fluency scores, for example, are below a particular criterion (e.g., the 20th percentile or DIBELS standards) and the rate of growth is less than one standard deviation below the average growth rate for the general population, then that student would be considered eligible for special education. The reason the DD approach is used rather than simply finding three data points below an aim line is because the aim line approach is used to judge effectiveness of interventions. Although there are no studies that examine the use of aim line decisions for entitlement purposes, there are several studies that suggest DD data significantly differentiate reading skills of children at risk for reading failure with and without a DD profile (Burns & Senesac, 2005; Speece & Case, 2001; Speece, Case, & Molloy, 2003). Moreover, the slope of the aim line is dependent on how low the student's scores were to begin with and how much time will elapse between baseline and target score. For example, a student whose median baseline score in January is 15 words correct per minute and whose end-of-year (May) goal is 55 words correct per minute would have a much steeper aim line than someone with a baseline score of 25 in which the intervention started in September. The former student would need to improve by 2.22 words correct per minute each week to stay on target, but the latter would only need to progress by .88 words correct per minute per week. Thus, the first student may make significantly more progress than the latter student, but still have three points below the aim line. Comparisons to aim line can be very useful for instructional decisions within tier 3, but entitlement decision such as special education eligibility should be made with the psychometrically more rigorous DD model.

Advocates for RTI suggest that it will be a way for students to receive assistance more quickly than through traditional approaches, but skeptics quickly point out that to go from tier 1 through tiers 2 and 3 and into special education may require 8–16 weeks, which is a much longer time frame than allowed for a traditional special education evaluation. Thus, we have to ask, What exactly constitutes an evaluation for special education eligibility? It is not the provision of interventions as students progress through the tiers. The three-tiered model is an intervention approach, not an assessment. The evaluation is the examining of student response data to make an eligibility determination. The three-tiered model will not begin when the student is referred, but will already be in place as a schoolwide intervention approach. After completing tier 3, a referral for special education determination could be made and *existing* student response data would be considered with additional data collected as needed. From this perspective, an individualized educational planning team should have no problem meeting local, state, and federal mandates for eligibility consideration timelines. However, if a referral for special education should arise for a student in tiers 1 or 2, then the school would have to decide if it is an appropriate referral and whether or not RTI data would be used.

CONCLUSION

One cannot discuss entitlement decisions without discussing the purpose of special education. To do so, ask yourself, "What is special education?" When asked this very question respondents give a variety of answers that often focus on intensive services and alternative placements. However, special education was originally defined in the 1975 special education mandate (P.L. 94-142), and continued to be in the latest revision of Individuals with Disabilities Education Act (IDEA) (2004), as "specialized instruction, at no cost to the parents or guardians, to meet the unique needs of a child with a disability." Arguably the aspect of that definition that we do best in education is the "at no cost to the parents or guardians." Special education has seemingly become categorical instruction to meet the needs of classes of disabilities. RTI is an attempt to return to the roots of special education by individualizing instruction for the unique needs of children. Moreover, special education in an RTI model becomes a service that is used to enhance learning for students. In other words, we continue to search for the intervention/instructional methodology that will lead to student success, and if that approach is so intensive that it cannot be delivered without the resources of special education services, then an individualized education plan is written when the student is determined to be entitled to those services.

Although the situation described above is how RTI should operate, most schools will not be ready for that level of decision making for quite some time. We thus suggest a progression of special education decision making that follows the implementation plan of the school district. Schools first use RTI as an intensive prereferral or screening model that may result in a traditional special education eligibility assessment for some students. This will continue for the first few years of the implementation process until the school district is sure that the model it is implementing is consistent with the RTI tiered intervention system and that what is implemented is actually what has been designed. Districts then evolve into using DD data for eligibility decisions. Finally, DD can be used for eligibility, but so could a positive trend in the data. In other words, a student who is unsuccessful in tier 3 would require special education services, which makes sense. However, a student who is successful in tier 3 may also be eligible for special education services if the intervention is too intense to be delivered without the financial resources that accompany an individualized education plan. RTI could result in an education that is truly special, but only if data are collected in a reliable manner, used in a manner that results in valid decisions, and then actually used to inform decisions about instruction, intervention, and entitlement.

4

Schoolwide Organization to Facilitate RTI

In order for a response-to-intervention (RTI) process to work effectively, schools must be organized such that problem solving does not exist in a vacuum, but is instead integrated into the overall system of communication and decision making in the school (Kameenui & Simmons, 1998). As shown in Table 4.1, schools that have successfully implemented RTI systems typically engage in three broad practices. First, they collect data regularly on all students to screen for difficulty. Data are collected more regularly for students who are at risk to determine if they are responding to well-designed instructional programs. Second, schools use empirically validated interventions and instructional practices within a multitiered service delivery model. Finally, schools are organized to ensure the most effective instruction possible for each student. Without a school-level system of implementation, it is nearly impossible for assessment-and-instruction best practices to be put into place effectively. The school as the "host environment" must be organized to ensure that research-based practices can thrive and be sustained (Coyne, Kameenui, & Simmons, 2001).

ELEMENTS OF RTI SCHOOLWIDE ORGANIZATION

This section will provide information on six elements of school organization that can assist in ensuring that effective instruction can be provided to all students:

1. continuous measurement
2. grade-level team meetings
3. grade-level scheduling
4. flexible grouping
5. concentrated resources
6. problem-solving teams

Table 4.1 Characteristics of Effective Problem-Solving Teams

Characteristics of Effective Teams	Rating	Evidence/Comments
1. Is there a school team designed to help *general education teachers and parents* solve student problems?	1 2 3 4 5	
2. Is the problem-solving team seen as a *general education rather than a special education process*?	1 2 3 4 5	
3. Does the team have *balanced representation* of grade-level, general, and special education staff?	1 2 3 4 5	
4. Is an *administrator a team member*?	1 2 3 4 5	
5. Are there *multiple problem-solving teams* when the size of the school outstrips the workload of one team?	1 2 3 4 5	
6. Is there a *regularly scheduled* meeting time and place?	1 2 3 4 5	
7. Does the team have an agreed-upon *mission statement*?	1 2 3 4 5	
8. Does the team have a *manual* of procedures, forms, and resources?	1 2 3 4 5	
9. Does the team have *forms* used at the meetings to lead the team through the problem-solving process?	1 2 3 4 5	
10. Are there flexible *roles* assigned to team members (e.g., timekeeper, facilitator, recorder, case manager)?	1 2 3 4 5	
11. Does the team use *effective communication* (e.g., open-ended questioning, reflective listening)?	1 2 3 4 5	
12. Is there a process for *notifying parents* and obtaining consent for problem solving?	1 2 3 4 5	
13. Are parents provided a *description of assurances* of what general-education problem-solving will provide (e.g., timelines, data to be collected, decision-making rules)?	1 2 3 4 5	
14. Are there standard procedures (i.e., *review, interview, observe, and test* procedures) that are used to collect problem-solving data?	1 2 3 4 5	

Table 4.1 (continued) Characteristics of Effective Problem-Solving
Teams

Characteristics of Effective Teams	Rating	Evidence/Comments
15. Is there a system with which *teachers can access* the team?	1 2 3 4 5	
16. Does the team *maintain records on students* served through the team?	1 2 3 4 5	
17. Are data regularly collected *on team functioning* (e.g., students served)?	1 2 3 4 5	

Continuous Measurement

A valid and reliable measurement system is critical to successful implementation of RTI systems. As stated in chapter 2, we suggest that all children in preschool through grade 8 be assessed three times each year. Students who are performing below target should be assessed more frequently as needed. Since measurement has already been described in previous chapters, we will not discuss it again here. It is included at this point only to emphasize its critical nature, as a necessary component to effective implementation of the model.

Grade-Level Team Meetings

Once schools are organized to measure student progress on a regular basis, the system needs to be organized so that teachers actually use the data to make instructional decisions. One way to accomplish this task is to have teams of grade-level teachers meet regularly to review student achievement data. At the St. Croix River Education District in Minnesota, school principals organize these meetings to occur at least three times per year; however, the majority of teams meet once per month. Often each classroom teacher considers the students in his class to be his sole responsibility. Through the grade-level team process, the goal is to have grade-level staff members collectively consider all students as one group to be supported together.

Several activities are completed during grade-level team meetings. First, shortly after each benchmark assessment, teams review data and evaluate the percentage of students that are at or above target (tier 1), somewhat below target (tier 2), or significantly below target (tier 3). Second, after reviewing the benchmark data, grade-level teams set goals for the percentage of students they would like to have performing at or above target by the end of the year. For example, if in the fall a fourth grade class had 68% of students performing at or above target, the team might establish a goal of having 75% of students performing at or above target by spring. To accomplish this task, grade-level teams are provided with a chart to display the numbers and percentages of students falling into each tier of performance, as well as the numbers moving across tiers, at each benchmark testing season (fall, winter, and spring). This chart is shown in Figure 4.1, and is known as the *summary of effectiveness chart*. It is also affectionately known as the "chutes and ladders" chart by school staff, as it reminds us of the popular children's game.

This chart is organized into nine boxes—one for each tier—within each benchmark season. To add emphasis, the boxes might have color backgrounds: green for tier 1 (labeled *Benchmark*), yellow for tier 2 (labeled *Strategic*), and red for tier 3 (labeled *Intensive*). The range of scores appears next to each label; for example, in the fall the target for *Benchmark* is 70 words correct per minute (WCM) and above, and the range for *Strategic* is from 38 up to but not including 70 WCM. These ranges represent the criteria for success that this school has decided upon based on the predictive link between these scores and success on the statewide assessment.

Third, grade-level teams discuss the programming they plan to provide to students in each tier group. For example, the team may discuss the organization of a 90-minute core reading block for all students, the specific contents of an additional 30 minutes of supplemental small-group instruction for all students below target, and possibly another more intensive plan for students in tier 3. Finally, grade-level teams typically meet monthly to review the progress of all students in tiers 2 and 3 and to discuss program changes that would increase success for all students. Program changes include changing allocated time, instructional groups, motivational strategies, activities, group size, and/or curriculum. Program effectiveness is evaluated in large part based on the extent to which students on a particular grade level stay on that grade level and the extent to which students below grade level are able to catch up.

Grade-Level Scheduling

Another aspect of schoolwide organization is the common scheduling of basic skills instruction within grade levels. For example, all grade 1 teachers may agree to teach reading from

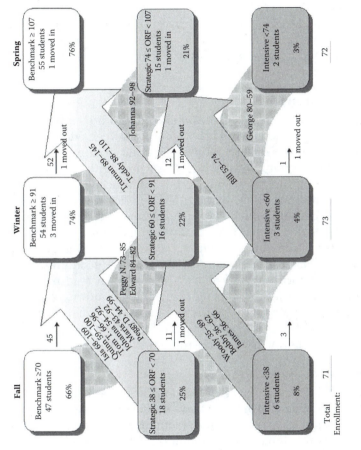

Figure 4.1 The Summary of Effectiveness Chart for the Problem-Solving Process.

9:30 to 11:00 each morning and math from 12:30 to 1:30 each afternoon. Setting up a schedule such as this for all grades requires some planning and coordination with regard to lunches, recesses, and special class schedules, but is entirely feasible within the context of a typical school schedule. In addition, we suggest that principals consider scheduling basic skills instruction at different times *across* grade levels. There are two primary benefits to this type of grade-level scheduling: first, it is possible that teachers may opt to create flexible instructional groups that are different from initial classroom assignments; second, it allows school-level resources to be concentrated at each grade level during the most opportune times each day.

Flexible Grouping

Once grade-level teams are established and a common basic skills block is scheduled, the teams may consider the use of flexible grouping procedures. Flexible grouping involves homogenous grouping of students according to achievement levels, but unlike traditional grouping procedures, students move in and out of groups regularly as determined by their progress. Because all teachers of a particular grade level teach the same instructional content at the same time each day, the possibility of flexibly regrouping across classrooms becomes available. For example, the few students in each classroom who are performing well above grade level in reading might be pulled together for a specific enrichment unit for a period of time. Alternatively, a group of students who are determined to need additional phonics instruction might be grouped to receive instruction at their current level of need.

Concentrated Resources

Another important facet of schoolwide organization is the notion of concentrating resources in an efficient and effective manner. In a day and age where resources are scarce, school districts are often forced to do more with either the same or fewer resources. A benefit of grade-level scheduling is the availability of concentrated resources (e.g., reading specialists, special education teachers, etc.) to each grade-level team. When each grade level has some unique period of the school day at which reading is taught, then all additional nonclassroom-based staff members can be assigned to support reading at that grade level during that time. This often includes special education, Title One, or paraprofessional staff members. If a school has five sections of grade 3, it may have access to an additional three or four staff members to assist with reading instruction during that instructional block. We suggest that school principals give grade-level teams the authority to decide as a group the best use for these additional resources.

Problem-Solving Teams

The last element of schoolwide organization necessary to ensure effective implementation of RTI is the formation of a school-level problem-solving team. While grade-level teams are able to solve many problems, they need a mechanism for obtaining additional assistance when they have exhausted their collective resources. We have enough experience working with schools to know that all have a variety of teams (e.g., student support teams, teacher assistance teams, student assistance teams, behavior support teams, etc.) that serve different purposes and include a wide variety of behavioral norms and activities completed (Burns, Vanderwood, & Ruby, 2005).

We suggest that each school form a problem-solving team (PST) whose primary function is to assist regular education teachers in meeting the needs of at-risk learners. A problem-solving team planning worksheet is included on the accompanying CD to assist schools in setting up teams. It is critical that the PST be viewed as a general education rather than special education process. On the grade-level team, teachers work to meet the needs of all children by utilizing grade-level resources. In instances where their efforts do not result in student success, a referral to the PST is made. Each school-based PST should follow a specific process for responding to identified student concerns. For PSTs to be effective, several characteristics of effective teamwork must be present. These are described in more detail in the next section.

CHARACTERISTICS OF EFFECTIVE TEAMS

Effective teams have a number of characteristics that contribute to their effectiveness. These characteristics can be sorted into five categories: group membership, group processes, standard procedures and documentation, procedures for parental involvement, and accurate record keeping and evaluation of team functioning. These characteristics are described in further detail in the following sections and are summarized in Table 4.1.

Group Membership

When forming a PST, care should be taken to ensure that there is balanced representation of grade-level staff. Larger schools may consider having more than one problem-solving team if the size of the school outstrips the workload of one team. For example, consider an elementary school of 900 students in grades K–6. This school may consider having one team for grades K–3 and another team for grades 4–6. In addition to balanced representation among grade levels, there should also be balanced representation of regular education and special education staff. If the primary membership of the PST is comprised of special education teachers, the team is likely to be viewed as a special education "hoop-jumping process." The PST must work to dispel the notion that referrals to the team will most likely end up with an evaluation for special education services. Once PSTs have been functioning successfully, this myth will naturally be dispelled as teachers in the school observe students making good success with interventions. Finally, an administrator (e.g., the principal or assistant principal) should be a team member. Because the school principal is the instructional leader in the building and is able to allocate resources, her participation on the team is critical. Moreover, the administrator has the capability to hold the team accountable for tasks and duties. Key personnel to involve in the PST include the referring teacher, the school psychologist, at least one other general education teacher, a special education teacher, and specialized personnel as needed (e.g., a social worker, a speech and language pathologist).

Group Processes

Once the PST is formed, a number of group process variables need to be considered. First, the team should have a mission statement that all team members agree upon. Second, the team should determine a regularly scheduled meeting time and place. We have seen schools schedule PST meetings before school, after school, and occasionally during the school day with substitute teachers provided to release classroom teachers from their usual duties. Each team will need to determine which option work best in their school, as there is no one-size-fits-all answer to scheduling. Third, flexible roles should be assigned to team members. These roles include that of facilitator, timekeeper, recorder, and case manager. The facilitator should organize an agenda with input from the team prior to each meeting, and the timekeeper ensures that the agenda is followed in a timely and efficient manner. The recorder keeps notes and/or documents the process on problem-solving forms. The case manager pulls together all information and coordinates the delivery and evaluation of the intervention. Finally, the team should use effective techniques such as open-ended questioning and reflective listening.

Collaboration is a process by which two professionals engage in a nonhierarchical relationship to develop interventions (Rosenfield, 1987) and is also a critical aspect of the group process within the PST. Collaboration in most PSTs is limited to conferences among a group of professionals, which is probably too limiting a role. A common procession of consultation within ineffective PSTs involves a frustrated teacher seeking consultation from the team, which then suggests interventions for the already frustrated teacher to attempt, followed by a referral to the school psychologist to determine special education eligibility and needs. Burns, Wiley, and Viglietta (in press) call this process a *shift in responsibility*—from the teacher to the team; back to the teacher; then temporarily to the school psychologist; and finally to a special education teacher or back to the frustrated teacher, depending on the results of the evaluation. However, if the PST process involves a *sharing* of responsibility, then collaboration can be more effective (Burns et al., in press). This sharing is best accomplished with immediate, supportive, effective, and lasting collaboration through the PST process shown in Figure 4.2. It is important that the referring teacher feel sufficiently supported in the implementation process and that collaborative efforts before and after a PST meeting reduce the length of time required at the meeting. The actual PST conference should require no more than 10–15 minutes for each child, as any additional time is usually spent "admiring" the problem rather than solving it (Allen & Graden, 2002, p. 568).

Standard Procedures and Documentation

The PST process is often seen as both vague and dynamic. Although the process is clearly not static, there is a sequence of steps that effective teams follow. Problem solving is the attempt to eliminate the difference between "what is" and "what should be" (Deno, 2002, p. 38). Thus, a successful PST process should closely follow the problem-solving stages of (1) problem identification, (2) problem analysis, (3) plan development, (4) plan implementation, and (5) plan evaluation.

Student Name:	Grade:	Gender: Female Male
Parent(s):	Referring Teacher:	Date of Referral:

Teacher Concern:	

Date of Initial Consultation:	Consultant:

Behaviorally Defined Problem:

Relevant Information From Cumulative File:

Relevant Information Obtained From Student:

Relevant Information Obtained From Parent(s):

Baseline Data:

Interventions Attempted Before PST Conference:

Date of PST Conferences: First _____ Second _____ Third _____

Second Intervention:

Person Responsible and Timeline:

Date of First Follow-Up:

Third Intervention:

Person Responsible and Timeline:

Date of Second Follow-Up:

Data:

_____
_____
_____

Figure 4.2   The Problem-Solving Team Data Collection Form (*Source:* Burns, Wiley, & Viglietta, in press.)

These stages involve specific activities that will be discussed in some detail in chapter 7.

Successful teams typically have a manual of procedures, forms, and resources that assist with the problem-solving process. Many school districts advocate for a common set of forms to be used at meetings to lead teams through the problem-solving process. Copies of sample forms are included on the accompanying CD. The purpose of the forms is not to create additional paperwork but to assist in documenting that the problem-solving process is carried out with integrity. School districts that use RTI to assist in making special education entitlement decisions must be able to document that problems were identified and analyzed, well-designed interventions were implemented with integrity and matched to student needs, and interventions were evaluated to determine whether they were successful.

Parental Involvement

We know that interventions are most successful when parents are involved early and often in the process (Englund, Luckner, Whaley, & Egeland, 2004). While school districts are not mandated to obtain parental permission for student interventions, best practices would suggest that a process exists for notifying parents and obtaining support for problem solving. Moreover, parents should be provided with assurances of what general education problem solving will provide (e.g., timelines, data to be collected, and decision-making rules). A sample parent brochure that explains the RTI process is included on the accompanying CD.

In addition to notification, parents should be invited to participate in PST meetings, share strategies that they have seen work with their children, and have some say in which intervention will be implemented. If parents do not attend, either the teacher or related service provider should interview them before the conference, and follow up with a communication home to inform the parent of what was discussed and what intervention was selected. It is also important that teams allow parents to exercise their due-process rights and request a traditional evaluation if they feel that one is necessary and that available data support the validity of such a request. However, in our experience parents are often satisfied with efforts to remedy the problem and drop such requests when successful interventions are found.

Systemic Interventions

PSTs have been linked to systemic outcomes such as reductions in the number of children referred to and placed into special education (Burns & Symington, 2002). Thus, PST should also focus on systemic issues as well as individual problems. For example, a PST may collect data regarding the number of student absences within a particular grade, low average grades or scores for a particular middle school subject or course, or a high frequency of students from a particular grade that do not obtain a proficient score on specific items from a state accountability test. Moreover, the PST should focus on systemic data of the PST itself because it is not unusual for schools to hastily implement a PST model and not include an evaluation component (Illback, Zins, Maher, & Greenberg, 1990). Thus, outcomes should also be examined, such as the number of students adequately responding to interventions, measures of teacher and parent satisfaction, and aggregated measures of individual student learning. Moreover, measures of school climate and other system variables (e.g., number of children considered for or retained) should be considered because these data may assist in determining tier 1 and tier 2 interventions.

Record Keeping and Evaluation of Team Functioning

Finally, PSTs need to maintain records on students served by the team. These data are important for a number of reasons. First, they aid in efficient transition when students move to different grades or different schools. When the process has been documented, future teachers have a record that documents what interventions have been tried in the past and the success of these interventions. Second, accurate records allow administrators to evaluate the functioning of the team along with the percentage of students referred for problem solving as well as the outcome of the problem solving. For example, let's suppose a middle school of 850 students had 10 students referred for problem solving in a school year. At the same time, benchmark data collected on all students indicate that only 60% of students are at or above district target scores. We know that there are likely many more than 10 students who are at risk for academic or behavioral difficulty, yet a systems problem exists in the fact that teachers are not accessing the PST for assistance. In this case, an analysis should be conducted to determine why teachers are not accessing the team and how well the team is functioning.

Implementation integrity provides the foundation for assessing student response within RTI (Noell & Gansle, 2007), and PSTs are often implemented without fidelity to the PS process (Burns et al., 2005). Thus, the forms provided in Figure 4.3 and Table 4.1 can be used to assess the fidelity of the process. These fidelity data can document how well the process is

Item	Yes	No
1. The team meets on a consistent (e.g., weekly) basis.		
2. A Request for Assistance Form (RAF) is used to identify problem and provide data before the meeting.		
3. The RAF is brief, but provides adequate information about the problem.		
4. There is documentation of consultant meeting with teacher prior to PST meeting.		
5. Baseline data are collected and presented.		
6. Data are objective and empirical.		
7. Selected interventions are research based.		
8. Selected intervention is directly linked to assessment data.		
9. Start with interventions that have a high probability of success.		
10. Consulting personnel assist with the implementation of intervention.		
11. The team develops a specific implementation plan with teacher.		
12. Parental information is discussed.		
13. A data-collection plan is developed to monitor effectiveness and progress.		
14. Monitoring data are objective, empirical, and directly linked to the problem.		
15. A plan is developed to assess implementation integrity of the intervention.		
16. A follow-up consultation is scheduled between teacher and one PST member.		
17. A follow-up meeting is scheduled.		
18. A case documentation form is used to track the team's activities.		
19. The school principal or administrative designee is present at the meeting.		
20. PST members have designated roles (e.g., note taker, discussion facilitator).		

Figure 4.3 The Problem-Solving Team Process Fidelity Checklist.

implemented should legal challenges occur and can be used to identify areas in need of ongoing professional development.

CONCLUSION

RTI requires that schools have supporting structures in place, such as frequent and continuous measurement, grade-level team meetings, flexible grouping procedures, grade-level scheduling, concentrated resources, and school-level problem-solving teams. This chapter has provided information on how schools can organize for success by incorporating these critical elements. Implementing RTI in a school or district can be an overwhelming proposition. However, putting these supporting structures in place will facilitate implementation and allow for enhanced learning for all students.

5

Tier 1:
Curriculum and Instruction for All Children

Batsche and colleagues (2006) noted that response-to-intervention (RTI) involves providing high-quality instruction and interventions matched to student need, monitoring progress frequently to make changes in instruction, and applying child response data to important educational decisions. It is no accident that high-quality instruction is listed first, because success in tiers 2 and 3 is quite predicated on an effective tier 1.

As was discussed in chapter 1, the roots of RTI can be traced to two documents: *Data-Based Program Modification* (Deno & Mirkin, 1977) and *A Nation at Risk* (U.S. Department of Education, 1983). Much of our book is dedicated to discussing how the former has affected education in this country, but this chapter will address the influence of the latter. Recommendations from *A Nation at Risk* address higher standards and expectations, academic content, student task engagement, teacher quality, and school leadership, but higher standards seems to be the area on which the public and future policy makers have focused (Wong, Guthrie, & Harris, 2004). As a result, despite potentially flawed methods and resulting conclusions, *A Nation at Risk* led to a shift from measuring educational quality with input (e.g., resources) to measuring output (i.e., student performance) for all student groups (Guthrie & Springer, 2004). This resulting assessment of student learning for all students eventually evolved into the accountability mandates of the No Child Left Behind Act of 2001.

The combination of higher standards and assessing outcomes has led to revised high school graduation requirements and more stringent content requirements (Guthrie & Springer, 2004). In other words, assessing output led to conversations about enhancing the process without increasing input (i.e., resources). There are clearly controversial issues associated with *A Nation at Risk* and the No Child Left Behind Act, but it is difficult to argue against the focus on results now commonplace in American education. Moreover, despite the shortcomings of both, this change appears to have had a lasting effect from which we can make positive outcomes occur for students. This chapter will discuss recent reforms in reading instruction, outline requirements for quality instruction, and present potential tier 1 interventions.

REFORMS IN READING INSTRUCTION

Methods for teaching children how to read have been a matter of some debate for the past several decades. The book *Why Johnny Can't Read* (Flesch, 1955) may have started the great debate, but it argued for the need for phonics instruction over teaching via memorization of whole words, which were much more comparable approaches than debated today. In the recent past, reading instruction focused on providing a literacy-rich learning environment in order to stress contextual meaning as a method to enhance reading skills (whole language). This was contrasted by a more code-base primary method of instruction in which children were taught letter sounds and how to sound out words.

Recent research has found that reading based on explicit instruction of phonological and alphabetic principles leads to faster rates of growth and better word recognition skills, but the effects are stronger for children with reading difficulties and less robust for general reading comprehension (Foorman, Francis, Fletcher, Schatschneider, & Mehta, 1998). More recently, the National Reading Panel (NRP) was created to review reading research and report a summary of research-based knowledge regarding reading instruction (U.S. Senate Committee on Appropriations, 1997). The findings of the NRP have noted that quality reading instruction involves teaching children to break apart and manipulate the sounds in words that are represented by letters of the alphabet, having students practice reading orally with close guidance, and applying strategies for better understanding what is read (NRP, 2000). Of course, many reading scholars favor a balanced literacy approach in which code strategies are taught in combination with meaning-based strategies using authentic texts (Pressley, 2005), but it seems that the NRP report (2000) placed at least a temporary hold on the reading debate. Although critics of NRP methods and findings continue to question many important aspects of the report, for now the debate has as close to a definitive conclusion as it is ever going to have.

QUALITY INSTRUCTION

Stein, Johnson, and Gutlohn (1999) have defined a quality reading curriculum as one that includes explicit phonics instruction and a strong relationship between the phonics instruction and the selection of words used in reading material. The latter is referred to as *decodable text*, a term that has unfortunately negative connotations that invoke memories of the unimaginative and uninteresting prose used in the *Dick and Jane* reading series. The term simply refers to curricular reading material that uses a high percentage of words made of sounds/letters that have been taught in preceding lessons. The review conducted by Stein et al. examines seven reading curricula that were published in 1996 and concludes that only two included explicit phonics instruction—one of which accomplished this with supplemental material. Moreover, seven curricula included connected text that involved approximately 33–50% of words that were not easily decodable and not made of previously instructed sounds (Stein et al., 1999). Thus, few curricula met the criteria of phonics instruction and decodable text.

A similar review of curricula conducted in 2004, but with curricula published between 1996 and 2000, found a range of decodable text from approximately 16% to approximately 70%, with four of the six curricula containing less than 50% decodable words and all six including anywhere from 15% to 55% of words that contained sounds that were never taught in the curriculum (Foorman, Francis, Davidson, Harm, & Griffin, 2004). Shanahan (2006) has reported that many publishers have revised curricula based on the findings of the NRP, and our own review of curricula would support that, but a systemic review much like those reported by Stein et al. (1999) and Foorman et al. (2004) has yet to be conducted.

Of course, explicit phonics instruction and decodable text are not the hallmark of all quality reading curricula across grades. The National Research Council has indicated that reading instruction in kindergarten and the first grade should focus on phonemic awareness and phonics instruction; in second grade on explicit phonics, writing, and reading fluency, and in third grade on reading fluency and reading comprehension

(Snow, Burns, & Griffin, 1998). However, an important shift occurs in fourth grade in that instruction moves from learning to read to reading to learn, which results in a focus on reading comprehension that lasts throughout the remaining grades, with focus on application to content areas in the high school years (Snow et al., 1998).

In addition to quality curricular materials and focused instruction, the National Research Council recommends that two hours each day be dedicated to reading instruction (Snow et al., 1998). Ninety minutes of reading intervention needs to occur in addition to core quality reading instruction. Moreover, reading instruction needs to include free-choice reading, word study, and writing. Each of these three will be discussed in more detail below.

Free-Choice Reading

When children engage in silent reading during classroom instruction, reading achievement increases (Taylor, Frye, & Maruyama, 1990). This finding has led to several sustained silent reading approaches with intuitive appeal such as Drop Everything and Read. The expected outcomes of sustained silent reading is increased motivation and engagement, but there is a limited research base to support this claim, and even the goal of teacher modeling is often unmet by students' not observing the teacher's behavior (Bryan, Fawson, & Reutzel, 2003). However, research has consistently found that providing an appropriate level of challenge in reading material leads to increased time on task and task completion (Gickling & Armstrong, 1978; Treptow, Burns, & McComas, 2007), which suggests that student engagement is enhanced by using appropriately challenging reading material. Thus, perhaps the first step in free-choice reading is to limit the choice to books that are readable at individual students' respective independent reading levels. After obtaining an appropriate reading level, allowing students to select reading material based on interest would seem to be a useful activity.

Providing appropriate material is only the first step; of equal importance is what is asked of the students during independent reading, because quantity in addition to quality reading leads to improved outcomes (Topping, Samuels, & Paul, 2007). Teachers should give students specific details for which to read during independent reading, ask higher-order questions about reading, and use social discourse during and after reading tasks. These approaches have led to improved student engagement and comprehension (Bryan et al., 2003; Taylor, Pearson, Clark, & Walpole, 2000).

Word Study

Walk into just about any elementary schoolroom and you will probably see a "word wall" on which various words have been written on large note cards and affixed in a decorative manner. Often these words are "red letter" words that cannot be sounded out with phonetic approaches. This is consistent with the first aspect of an effective word study—that is, learning phonetically irregular and/or high-frequency words.

After learning appropriate sound-symbol relationships, the unit of interest becomes the word. Students should then be taught to blend and segment sounds into words (which will be discussed below) and to recognize common and/or irregular words with little effort. It is likely that the best method to teach recognition of these words is through a system of frequent opportunities to respond (repetition) in an appropriately challenging way. One method to accomplish this is with *incremental rehearsal* (Tucker, 1989), in which the new word is rehearsed with previously acquired words that can be orally read within 2 seconds. The new word is presented up to nine times with gradually increasing known words between presentations (e.g., first new word, first known word, first new word, first known word, second known word, first new word, first known word, second known word, third known word, first new word, first known word, second known word, third known word, fourth known word, etc.—until anywhere from five to nine known words are used). Research has consistently demonstrated improved retention and generalization into contextual reading of words learned with incremental rehearsal (Bunn, Burns, Hoffman, & Newman, 2005; Burns, 2002; Burns, 2007; Burns, Dean, & Foley, 2004; MacQuarrie, Tucker, Burns, & Hartman, 2002). However, meta-analytic research has found that any rehearsal model that contains at least 50% known words leads to strong effects (Burns, 2004), which suggests that less time-consuming approaches were effective for most students as long as a high percentage of known items and frequent repetition of new ones were included.

The second aspect of a word study involves segmenting and blending sounds into words. Word sorts (Bear, Invernizzi, Templeton, & Johnston, 1996) are a common approach to the former, and word boxes (Clay, 1993) are frequently used for the latter. Word boxes involve analyzing parts of words by first segmenting sounds and then blending sounds together to form whole words. Usually the student is presented with magnetic letters representing the sounds of a word with boxes above them representing the number of sounds in a word (e.g., *dog* would have three boxes with the three letters *d*, *o*, and *g* beneath each box). The student states the word orally, then restates each individual sound while sliding the corresponding letter into its corresponding ordinal position within the boxes (e.g., the letter *d* into the first box); and finally, the student restates the blended word.

Word sorts study words by having students make word analogies or categorize words that share common elements such as sounds or spelling patterns. In this approach the student is presented with a series of note cards containing 15 words. These words might be explicitly grouped into three categories based on sounds. For example, the student can be taught to discriminate short vowels, long vowels that end in *e*, and long vowels with an *ai* diagraph by giving five examples of each and one model for each. In this case the student would be shown one example of each, have the first row modeled, and sort the remaining cards into the three categories, as shown in Figure 5.1. Both word boxes and word sorts have been shown to be effective in increasing word recognition and spelling (Joseph, 1998–99, 2000; Santa & Hoien, 1999).

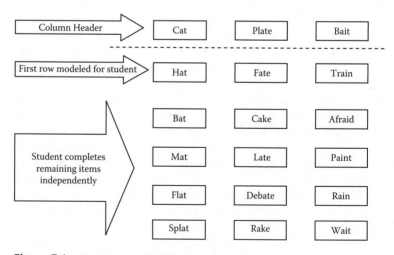

Figure 5.1   An Example of a Word Sort.

Writing

Written expression is a skill composed of five hierarchical and interrelated subskills including mechanics, production, conventions, linguistics, and cognition (Bradley-Johnson & Lesiak, 1989). The *mechanics* of written expression include letter formation and handwriting, while *production* refers to the number of words, sentences, and paragraphs a student writes. Writing *conventions* include capitalization, punctuation, and spelling rules. *Linguistics* refers to the use of correct syntax and varied vocabulary. *Cognition* considers the coherent, logical, and sequential organization of written text.

Until grade 4, the emphasis for writing instruction is on the mechanics, production, and conventions of writing, and students who struggle with writing most often have difficulties with skills lower on the hierarchy such as mechanics and production (Berninger, Mizokawa, & Bragg, 1991). However, a survey of practices even among teachers of older students has found more time devoted to teaching the lower end of the hierarchy and less to teaching the writing processes such as planning, revising, and text organization (Graham & Harris, 2005). Of course, much like reading, a balanced approach to writing instruction is likely best (Graham, Berninger, Abbott, Abbott & Whitaker, 1997).

Phases of Instruction

In addition to areas for instruction, individual lessons should also follow a carefully planned sequence of activities to ensure the best possible outcome. Algozzine and Ysseldyke (1992) have presented a model of effective instruction that includes (1) planning, (2) managing, (3) delivering, and (4) evaluation. Each will be discussed below along with corresponding activities.

Planning Instruction

Effective instruction begins with instructional planning, which involves deciding what to teach, how to teach it, and how to best communicate realistic expectations to the class and to individual students (Algozzine, Ysseldyke, & Elliott, 1997). More specifically, this involves establishing goals for learning, assessing gaps between current skill and expected performance, and determining an appropriate pace for instruction by assessing student behaviors (e.g., skill levels and motivation), task characteristics (e.g., sequence and cognitive demands), and classroom characteristics (e.g., instructional groupings and materials; Ysseldyke & Burns, in press). Thus, effective teachers are aware of what skills their students have already mastered and how student skills and deficits interact with the learning task demands, material, and environment.

Managing Instruction

There are three principles of managing instruction: (1) preparation, (2) using time productively, and (3) establishing a positive classroom environment (Algozzine et al., 1997). Preparation of instruction involves long-term activities such as setting rules, practicing procedures, and establishing consequences for behavior, but also involves directly preparing students for an upcoming instructional unit or lesson through preteaching activities.

Productive use of time is a central concept to effective teaching because students need ample opportunities to respond to academic and other classroom tasks (Carroll, 1963). Although well-managed instructional environments involve established routines and procedures, organized physical space, short transitions between activities, a task-oriented focus, and allocation of sufficient time to academic activities (Ysseldyke & Algozzine, 1995), the essential attribute of effective classes could very well be that time is conserved by planning activities and tasks to fit learning materials (Evertson & Harris, 1992). Teaching children at their individual instructional levels has consistently led to increased skill, but is also linked to increased task completion and time on task (Burns & Dean, 2005; Gickling & Armstrong, 1978; Treptow et al., 2007).

Delivering Instruction

After being carefully planned, instruction is effectively delivered if it is well presented; this involves providing relevant practice, keeping the students interested and motivated, and providing feedback. There needs to be sufficient controlled (guided) and independent (seatwork or homework) practice to optimize student achievement (Algozzine & Ysseldyke, 2006). Although many might suggest that it is critical to use creative and varied methods when providing practice, it is equally important to provide sufficient opportunities to respond to the learning stimuli and to stay with that practice until mastery has occurred. Research has consistently demonstrated that incorporating review and known material while independently rehearsing target items leads to increased retention of the items (MacQuarrie et al., 2002), increased preference for the task (Skinner, Hall-Johnson, & Skinner, 1999), and increased time on task during the activity (Treptow et al., 2007). Thus, knowing which items in a learning task represent new versus review material may be as important as presenting those items in a novel manner.

Finally, it is essential that students receive information about the quality of their performance and the extent to which they are performing in accordance with expectations. Meta-analytic research has consistently linked feedback provided to students with academic achievement (Azevedo & Bernard, 1995; Rawshorne & Elliott, 1999; Swanson, 1999). Thus, effective teaching involves giving students immediate, frequent, and explicit feedback on their performance and behavior (Algozzine & Ysseldyke, 2006). This may even be accomplished with verbal feedback from the teacher regarding the accuracy of the work and what specific errors have occurred (VanDerHeyden & Burns, 2005).

Evaluating Instruction

The final stage of instruction is self-evident among data-based decision makers and involves deciding whether the approaches, methods, and materials used have been effective. Areas that should be examined include student understanding, amount of engaged time, and student activity in order to create records of the performance and to make instructional decisions (Algozzine et al., 1997). Goals established in the planning phase should be explicitly stated, as students do not always identify goals that are consistent with those outlined by the teacher (Winne & Marx, 1982), and progress toward those goals should be closely monitored in the evaluating stage. Curriculum-based measurement data are uniquely appropriate for evaluating instruction.

Effective Practices in Schools

We are using an artificial delineation in order to organize this chapter into a more readable framework by discussing curriculum, instruction, and practices separately. Clearly the three belong under one comprehensive umbrella, but we divide them up to make three shorter sections for clarity within each. In addition to research-based curriculum and instruction, there are other practices in which successful schools engage, which will be further discussed below.

There is an extensive literature on effective schools (Levine & Lezotte, 1990; Lezotte, 1991, 2001) that consistently finds seven correlates of effective schools (Lezotte, 1991):

1. a clear school mission
2. high expectations
3. instructional leadership from the principal
4. time on task
5. a safe and orderly environment
6. positive home-school relationships
7. frequent monitoring of student progress

One of the best displays of these principles can be found in a recent series of newspaper articles in the St. Paul, Minnesota, *Pioneer Press*. A regression formula was used within this special report series to predict how many students in a school would score proficiently on the state accountability test given the percentage of them within the school who were eligible for the federal free or reduced lunch (FRL) program (Sylwester, 2006). For example, if 70% of the student population was eligible for FRL, then 60% would score proficiently, but 80% in the FRL would result in 60% scoring proficiently. The newspaper then reported on schools with at least 60% of students eligible for FRL whose students consistently scored proficiently on the state accountability test at a higher rate than was predicted for that school. In other words, these were schools that were successful despite working with a high-needs student population.

After identifying these "schools that work" (Boldt, 2006), teachers were interviewed as to how they beat the odds. Five common themes emerged including (1) emphasizing reading above all else, (2) providing support services beyond classroom instruction, (3) continuous assessment and small group instruction, (4) having an effective staff, and (5) having a structured, disciplined environment (Rx for Ailing Schools, 2006). These themes are consistent with the literature on effective schools and suggest that schools may need to consider adopting a research-based curriculum, utilize effective instructional practices within an orderly climate with well-trained staff, and consider services external to the classroom in order to meet the interrelated academic and social needs of all students. Doing so will result in enhanced student learning through an effective tier 1.

INTERVENTIONS

As in tiers 2 and 3, interventions are needed for tier 1. However, the focus of the intervention is the classroom and the group of students rather than individual students. Chapter 3 discusses how to assess if a tier 1 intervention is needed. Here we will discuss what a tier 1 intervention should entail.

As is always the case, the first step is the collection of data (detailed in chapter 3). The focus of data collection should be on student outcomes, but assessing the instructional environment may also provide relevant data with tier 1. Two commercially prepared measures provide useful information that can be obtained in a nonthreatening manner. The *Ecobehavioral Assessment System Software* (EBASS; Greenwood, Carta, Kamps, & Delquadri, 1995) and the *Functional Assessment of Academic Behavior* (FAAB; Ysseldyke & Christenson, 2002) both allow consultants to examine instructional practices from a problem-solving perspective. The combination of this information with student outcome data will suggest if an intervention is needed and directly suggest areas in which to intervene.

Many tier 1 interventions will involve changes in instructional practice as identified by ecological data, but sometimes student outcomes for the class remain low despite sound general instruction. In these cases classwide peer tutoring (Greenwood, Carta, & Hall, 1988) can be used to remediate basic skills. The key elements of a peer tutoring lesson for basic skills (e.g., letter sounds, math facts, etc.) are instructional-level skill practice with multiple massed opportunities to respond at a brisk pace with immediate corrective feedback, independent timed practice, and progression to the next skill level contingent on meeting a mastery criterion on the lower level skill (VanDerHeyden & Burns, 2005). The teacher's role in this intervention is to monitor the intervention to ensure high engagement and accurate implementation of procedures by the students.

Training teachers to implement a tier 1 intervention such as classwide peer tutoring involves the following sequence of activities based on the intervention model presented within the System to Enhance Educational Performance (STEEP; VanDerHeyden, Witt, & Naquin, 2003). First, the steps of the intervention are provided to the teachers in writing and role-played with a consultant. Next, a trained coach is assigned to the classroom on the first day to assist with correct implementation of the intervention sequence and with training the students in how to perform the intervention. Following training, teachers perform the intervention 4 days per week while also administering assessment probes of the single skills each day and multiskill progress-monitoring probes at least weekly. Finally, teachers are trained to move children to the next highest skill level in the relevant instructional sequence on the following day given a mastery level score during the daily timed assessment.

Peer-assisted learning strategies (PALS) in reading (Fuchs, Fuchs, & Burish, 2000) have been used within an RTI framework to deliver a classwide intervention with success (McMaster, Fuchs, Fuchs, & Compton, 2005) and are available at limited cost (approximately $60–$75 for each grade) online at www.kc.vanderbilt.edu/pals. PALS has been conceptualized as a tier 2 intervention in which students are tutored by peers in small groups on basic reading skills. However, McMaster and Wagner (2007) provide an example of using PALS as a tier 1 intervention in which peer tutoring was implemented three times per week for 35 minutes per session. Specific PALS activities include letter-sound recognition, decoding, sight word recognition, and fluency building. Basic to the PALS approach is the use of heterogeneous groupings in which the more skilled reader first serves as tutor or "coach" to the less-skilled "reader" (McMaster & Wagner, 2007), but the roles switch through reciprocal teaching throughout the lesson. The coach, regardless of which student in the dyad that may be, provides prompts, praise, and corrective feedback to the reader.

CONCLUSION

Tier 1 is vitally important because it affects every student and allows approximately 80% of the student population to successfully reach learning objectives. This can best be accomplished by selecting a reading curriculum that is consistent with the findings of the NRP (2000), by providing 2 hours of reading instruction each day that involves developmentally appropriate activities (e.g., phonics in early elementary school, reading comprehension strategies in later elementary and middle school, and content-area reading in high school), by using well-planned instructional sequences, and by addressing the social needs of the students. Moreover, whether or not these components are in place should be assessed and intervention undertaken as needed using objective measures such as the

EBASS and the FAAB. Finally, tier 1 interventions such as the peer-tutoring approaches used by the STEEP and the PALS could assist in enhancing student learning. After assuring a quality instruction in tier 1, students who do not meet criteria on benchmark assessments can then be confidently recommended for tier 2 interventions knowing that more intense assistance is needed.

6

Tier 2:
Intervention Strategies for a Selected Group

Approximately 20% of students will not be successful in general education instruction despite a quality core curriculum and instruction, and they will require a more intensive intervention. However, finding effective interventions for as many as 100 or more children (with, for example, 500 children in a school) is not practical nor logistically possible given the available resources in most schools; this suggests the need for an intermediate step between general education instruction and intensive individualized interventions. Providing this intermediate step will allow for efficient resource allocation while assuring student success in tier 2, but will also greatly enhance the efforts of tier 3 because the number of children requiring the level of analysis and intervention required for success will be decreased.

Tier 2 interventions are best delivered through small-group instruction and by using what are commonly referred to as *standard protocol interventions.* The term *standard protocol* can be somewhat misleading because it does not necessarily imply that every child receives the same intervention. In fact, matching student skill to intervention is just as important in tier 2 as it is in tier 3, but it has to be done in a more efficient manner, and with data, as discussed in chapter 3. Standard, in this case, refers to a common intervention for small groups of chidren to directly address a particular skill deficit. This chapter will discuss how to organize small groups and will suggest several interventions.

ORGANIZING SMALL GROUPS

Group Size

Meta-analytic research has found that small-group instruction is at least as effective as one-on-one interventions and perhaps more effective and more efficient (D'Agostino & Murphy, 2004; Elbaum, Vaughn, Tejero, & Watson, 2000; Vaughn, Gersten, & Chard, 2000). Thus, the ideal group size for tier 2 interventions appears to be four to six students because it combines effectiveness and efficiency. The more important question is not how many children should be in the tutor-tutee ratio, but who the tutor should be. Several options are available, including a fully licensed teacher, an educational assistant/paraprofessional, peer tutors, or volunteer tutors. It makes the most intuitive sense for a classroom teacher to deliver the tier 2 intervention, but expertise in the academic area (e.g., reading) is more important than status as the classroom teacher. Using a licensed teacher is comparatively the most costly option, but should lead to higher assurances of instructional quality. Thus, teacher involvement through supervision and/or curriculum and materials development is critical.

Peer tutors and adult volunteers are intriguing options for tier 2, and research has supported both within this model (Burns & Senesac, 2005; McMaster, Fuchs, Fuchs, & Compton, 2005). Tutors may also include much older students, or paraprofessionals, or parent volunteers. It must be emphasized, though, that any tutor serving in an instructional role needs to have proper training and ongoing oversight of a teaching professional.

The Length of Intervention

Interventions within tier 2 should be at least 30 minutes in length (except for the case of kindergarten students, who may be successful with 15- to 20-minute interventions) and should occur three to five times each week. It is important to note that this 30 minutes is in addition to—not instead of—90 minutes of reading instruction that occurs in general education. Equally important is the duration of the intervention. A minimum of 16 data points at two assessments per week are needed in order to provide reliable slopes with which judgments of student progress can be made (Christ, 2006). Therefore, if data are collected twice each week, a total of 8 weeks' worth of data would be needed. More weeks would be needed if data are collected on a less frequent basis.

Scheduling

Perhaps the main concern teachers and principals express when they begin implementing response-to-intervention (RTI) is the schedule. How can we possibly fit 30 minutes into the day for tier 2? Several options exist, and none is inherently better or worse than the others. However, some options work better within particular systems. Thus, listed below are three commonly used approaches along with advantages and disadvantages of each.

Within the Classroom

By far the easiest option for tier 2 is displayed in Figure 6.1. In this approach, a classroom with 25 students would probably include approximately 5 students (20%) that require a tier 2 intervention. In this case, the 20 remaining students would be assigned independent reading under the supervision of a paraprofessional, and the classroom teacher would deliver the 30-minute intervention to that small group.

This within-the-classroom approach would be undertaken every day, in some form, in just about every classroom. Teachers could frequently pull small groups of children aside often without the aid of a paraprofessional to supervise the remaining children. This approach would also allow for flexible grouping within the classroom in that students could join and exit the group quite easily, but limits the availability for multidisciplinary collaboration and flexible grouping across grades, classrooms, and skills. For example, if each of the five students in the example lacks phonetic skills, then this would

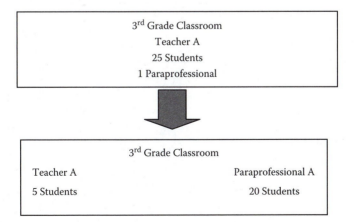

Figure 6.1   An Example of Tier 2 within the Classroom.

work. However, if one required a phonemic awareness intervention and two required fluency interventions, then this one-
size-fits-all approach would not be successful.

Schoolwide RTI Time

The second example, shown in Figure 6.2, works when the
school chooses to schedule the tier 2 intervention at a common time within the building. For example, every classroom
would have its tier 2 intervention from 2:30 to 3:00, and those
children not receiving tier 2 would participate in independent reading or some other mostly independent learning task
(e.g., centers). In Figure 6.2, there are two grade 3 classrooms
with 25 students in each. Thus, each would probably have
5 students (20%) who require a tier 2 intervention. Assuming
a common number for ease of demonstration, all six elementary grades would result in a total of 60 students participating
in tier 2, which would result in the need for 12 small groups
with 5 students in each, or perhaps 10 groups with 6 students
in each. One of the classroom teachers for each grade would
then supervise the remaining 40 students while the other led
a small-group intervention. Simple math dictates that this will
only covers 50% of the small groups, which means additional
staff will be needed, such as Title One teachers, reading specialists, paraprofessionals, or even school psychologists. It

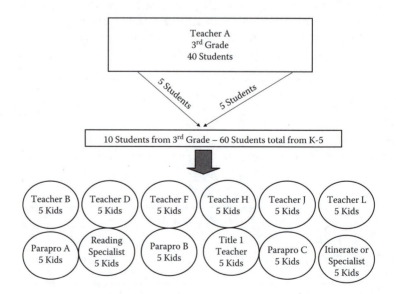

Figure 6.2   An Example of Schoolwide RTI Time.

may be possible to eventually have special education teachers lead a small group because up to 15% of special education resources can now be used for prevention and early intervention services. However, special education involvement in tier 2 can happen only after caseloads are reduced to a point that 30 minutes per day can be allocated to this service while still meeting the needs of children with disabilities.

Schoolwide RTI time offers many advantages. First, this allows for extensive grouping across grades in which true flexible skill grouping could occur. Second, it is less logistically confusing and easier for teachers to track. It allows for teachers to specialize in particular sets of interventions (e.g., phonics interventions), but they still could rotate responsibilities to learn different skills. Third, this could also allow time for enhanced learning opportunities for a school's gifted and talented students. Perhaps the biggest disadvantage would be the need for extensive collaboration. In this model one grade level could have students in as many as 10 different groups! That is highly unlikely, but it is possible. Regardless, there would likely be many different professionals involved in the education of a handful of children. While the advantages of collaboration are obvious, they also bring the need for communication that might not be possible in a typical school day. Moreover, this approach disrupts the general education classroom because students need to be grouped and supervised. However, we suggest that school personnel devise a more creative and subtle name other than Schoolwide RTI.

Floating RTI

The third commonly used model involves one or two specialists who work with various groups of children throughout the day. An example is provided in Figure 6.3, in which two specialists would be needed for 30-minute increments throughout the day. Both would operate a small group with about five students each, starting with the grade 1 at 9:30, then moving to kindergarten at 10:30, second grade at 11:00, and third grade at 1:30. This would also allow time to work with upper elementary students in a similar fashion.

The floating approach represents the middle group of the three options for tier 2 presented here on many important issues. First, it is easier to implement than the schoolwide RTI time model, but would not be quite as easy as the within-the-classroom approach. Comparably, the floating approach would require considerably fewer resources than the schoolwide

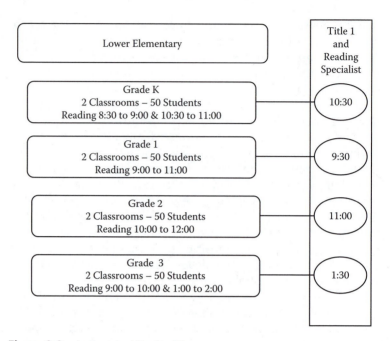

Figure 6.3   An Example of Floating RTI.

model, but would require probably at least two dedicated teachers, which is more than the within-the-classroom program needs. Moreover, a similar approach is probably already being conducted in most schools through remedial services such as Title One. However, simply calling Title One "tier 2" is probably not appropriate unless students are identified for Title One services with the data-based approaches described in chapters 2 and 3. Finally, floating RTI allows for flexible skill grouping within a grade, but *only* within the grade. This will probably be acceptable given that reading skills, and subsequent deficits, often follow a developmental pattern of phonemic awareness to phonics, to fluency, and to vocabulary/comprehension.

Secondary Schools

Generally speaking, middle schools and high schools have mostly been left out of the RTI conversation, with a few notable exceptions (e.g., the Illinois *Alliance for School-based Problem Solving and Intervention Resources in Education; the* St. Croix River Education District in Minnesota; the Chester County, Pennsylvania, school system). Thus, what RTI should look like at the secondary level is still a matter of some debate. Listed below are two examples of how tier 2 could work within a high or middle school.

The Traditional Schedule

A vast majority of tier 2 interventions at the secondary level involve some form of remedial course. In this model, a remedial reading course could be offered to students who fail or are likely to fail (as determined by curriculum-based measurement data) a state accountability test. Often, middle and high school days consist of six to eight periods of 50 to 60 minutes each, and one of those six to eight periods could be a remedial reading course for students experiencing difficulty. There is some research to support this, but it could be problematic for a few reasons. First, and perhaps most important, this model does not allow for flexible grouping in any way. Students would take the course for an entire semester or school year, but would not be able to easily exit the course into another one midsemester. Moreover, with only one teacher and 20 to 30 students, the possibility of small-group and individualized instruction is not likely. Some have suggested (and use) a more generic course, such as study skills, with smaller class sizes, but this still does not allow for easy transitions back and forth with other courses.

Alternatively, many schools use a content area such as social studies to deliver remedial reading instruction. The course would use the same curriculum as would a general social studies course and would use those materials to teach reading strategies. However, this approach calls for two teachers—one who is a content-area specialist and one who is a reading or intervention specialist. Moreover, this course would be limited to about 12–14 students because that would allow for half of the students to receive small-group instruction in reading and half in social studies for 25 to 30 minutes at the beginning of the period, and then the groups would switch for the remaining 25 to 30 minutes.

Ideally, students would be receiving small-group instruction in both reading strategies and content, which would increase skills in both. Thus, students should be able to smoothly transition back and forth between the remedial and general social studies courses with little disruption. However, this approach is somewhat resource intensive because it requires two teachers for 12–14 students.

The Block Schedule

Secondary schools are increasingly using block schedules in which periods last for 90 minutes and rotate on a more frequent basis. Although this presents a more complex scheduling system, there is some support for this model for improving student learning.

The block schedule can also make tier 2 easier to implement on one hand, but more difficult on the other. With 90 minutes of instruction, the possibility exists for three small groups of 5, 6, or perhaps even 7 students in each. Therefore, the size of the class can go from 12–14 (standard) to as many as 21 students with two teachers. The reading groups would remain at 5–7 students each, but the small-group content area (e.g., social studies) instruction would use groups of 10–14, which still likely represents a smaller student-to-teacher ratio than a general course and is still small enough to be effective. The primary difficulty is the rotating of courses; thus, in one school year this remedial approach may involve social studies, history, and earth science.

It is important to note that these suggested models do not emphasize reading over content-area knowledge. However, schools are being increasingly pressured to have their students pass state accountability tests, which become more content-area focused in secondary schools, and often the best intervention to increase the likelihood that a student will pass a state test in social studies, for example, is to increase her reading skills. Moreover, remedial instruction in the content area and in reading strategies using content-area materials further emphasizes the importance of this knowledge while simultaneously improving tests scores. Research on the use of RTI at the secondary level is just beginning, but contains quite promising results (Windram, Scierka, & Silberglitt, 2007).

Elements for Success

As has been stated earlier, not every model will work in every system, but one will likely work better than others. However, there are some core elements that facilitate success in every system. First, grade-level (in elementary schools) or content-area (in secondary schools) planning time is needed on at least a monthly basis. Ideally, teachers and relevant itinerate staff would meet once per week—and certainly no less than monthly—to review student data, discuss student difficulties, and collaborate on interventions. Other less-instructional issues can also be discussed during this time, but the focus should be on the review of data. Grade-level common instructional time is also needed in which all classrooms within one grade can teach reading at the same time. We find it somewhat surprising how infrequently a common grade-level reading time is used given the numerous advantages, but this is clearly a prerequisite for the floating RTI model, and makes the other models much easier.

Resources should be assigned to grade levels rather than classrooms and should be perceived as assigned in such a manner. For example, a classroom assistant (paraprofessional, educational assistant, etc.) is often assigned to a class for a certain period of the day. Some schools are fortunate enough to have an assistant for every classroom, but most are not. If there are three paraprofessionals assigned to three different classrooms within the same grade for 50% of the school day each, then that resource should be allocated as 1.5 full-time equivalents (or three half-day increments) to the grade rather than dividing them up by classroom. This may result in one classroom having an assignment of .80 because of more needy students and the other two having assignments of .35 each. Moreover, this will allow for flexible use of resources without taking time away from one particular classroom.

Finally, staff and administrators should be encouraged to be creative. Almost every school universally sees scheduling and resource logistics as the largest obstacles to tier 2 and to RTI in general. All we can say at this point is that every school with which we have worked has successfully tackled these problems. Adhering to these elements and working within an identified tier 2 model makes the transition easier, but staff will need to work together as problem solvers on the little issues and should be encouraged to do so.

INTERVENTIONS

Fortunately, the knowledge base on human learning is well informed, and meta-analytic research has identified several successful interventions. Thus, there are numerous potential instructional methodologies for tier 2, but selecting the appropriate ones is the challenge. Educators are constantly bombarded with conference presentations and marketing catalogs that all espouse research-based interventions. Burns (2006) have suggested that interventions selected for tier 2 should result in at least a moderate effect size while being easy to implement (manualized) and cost effective. A school district could spend a great deal of money and commit tremendous resources to a particular intervention, but if it is only slightly more effective than a cheaper one or one that requires minimal resources, then those saved funds and time could be allocated somewhere else, such as for curricula and training that might enhance learning for all students.

It does not matter how effective the program is if it is not implemented correctly. Thus, many school districts spend a great deal of money on commercially prepared interventions programs because they are usually easier to implement, have technical support, and claim a research base. Although the final claim is often debatable, the first two suggest a clear advantage. Schools should explicitly state what they do in tier 2 so that the methodologies can be easily transferable between teachers, assessed for implementation integrity, and presented to interested stakeholders. Moreover, if RTI data are used for eligibility decisions and one of those decisions is challenged in a hearing or court case, the school will need to be able to clearly document what it does and how well it does it.

Although commercially prepared programs and the subsequent manuals and materials are inviting, they are not necessary. Additionally, schools should look closely at the intervention program being sold to make sure it is research based and worth the cost. A recent review of research suggests that interventions are research based, and likely to be successful, if they are correctly targeted and provide explicit instruction in the skill, an appropriate level of challenge, sufficient opportunities to respond to and practice the skill, and immediate feedback on performance (Burns, VanDerHeyden, & Boice, in press). Thus, these could be used as criteria with which to judge potential tier 2 interventions.

Perhaps the most important point listed above is that the intervention be correctly targeted because one that lacks a different component (e.g., immediate feedback) may still be somewhat successful, but those that address the wrong skill have no hope of effectiveness. The work of the National Reading Panel (2000) can inform practice in tier 2. Once the deficit is correctly identified using data (as discussed in chapter 3), the student can receive the appropriate phonemic awareness, phonics, fluency, or vocabulary/comprehension intervention. Fortunately, the National Reading Panel has identified several effective interventions for each one, as identified by Shanahan

Table 6.1   Intervention Resources for National Reading Panel Areas

Resource	Cost*
Phonemic Awareness	
Ericson, L., & Juliebo, M. F. (1998). The phonological awareness handbook for kindergarten and primary teachers. Newark, DE: International Reading Association.	$18.95
Opitz, M. F. (2000). Rhymes and reasons: Literature and language play for phonological awareness. Portsmouth, NH: Heinemann.	$19.50
Phonics	
Bear, D. R., Invernizzi, M., Templeton, S., & Johnston, F. (2007). Words their way (4th ed.). Upper Saddle River, NJ: Prentice-Hall.	$37.95
Cunningham, P. M. (2004). Phonics they use: Words for reading and writing (4th ed.). New York: Allyn and Bacon.	$23.00
Lynch, J. (1998). Easy lessons for teaching word families. New York: Scholastic.	$14.95
Reading Fluency	
Blevins, W. (2001). Building fluency: Lessons and strategies for reading success. New York: Scholastic.	$13.99
Johns, J. L., & Berglund, R. L. (2006). Fluency: Strategies and assessment (3rd ed.). Dubuque, IA: Kendall-Hunt.	$29.95
Rasinski, T. V. (2003). The fluent reader. New York: Scholastic.	$20.99
Vocabulary and Comprehension	
Blachowicz, C., & Fisher, P. (2005). Teaching vocabulary in all classrooms (3rd ed.). Upper Saddle River, NJ: Prentice-Hall.	$30.00
Block, C. C., Gambrell, L. B., & Pressley, M. (Eds.). (2002). Improving comprehension instruction: Rethinking research, theory, and classroom practices. San Francisco: Jossey-Bass.	$36.00
Harvey, S., & Goudvis, A. (2007). Strategies that work: Teaching comprehension for understanding and engagement. Portland, ME: Stenhouse.	$30.00

* Cost determined by publisher websites in July 2007.
Source: Shanahan (2006).

(2006) and displayed in Table 6.1. It should be noted that all of these meet the criteria listed above and are relatively inexpensive. Thus, schools need only rely on solid instructional principles delivered in a small group rather than purchase an expensive program. However, programs should also be examined to judge which area they target. For example, we have seen many districts use the fluency intervention associated with Read Naturally (2004) as a tier 2 intervention with only limited success. That is because Read Naturally is a fluency intervention and is quite effective for children who lack fluency skills, but has only limited affect on phonemic awareness, phonics, and reading comprehension. Additionally, the Orton-Gillingham intervention (Gillingham & Stillman, 1997) is a well-researched one that primarily focuses on phonemic awareness and phonics, but if the child lacks reading fluency it likely will not have the same benefit.

CONCLUSION

Tier 2 seems to have a cloud of mystery around it because its importance is frequently emphasized, but there are few widely available examples from which to learn and model. Fortunately, tier 2 is not difficult if a model is implemented with fidelity, data are used to target interventions, cost-efficient and effective interventions are used, groups are limited in size to six students, interventions are attempted for 8 weeks, progress is closely monitored, and the elements for success are followed. Doing so will enhance student learning in tier 2 and allow for the more resource-intensive and in-depth analysis that occurs in tier 3 to be successful.

7

Tier 3:
Intensive Interventions for Individual Students

Research has found that despite best efforts, approximately 5% of the student population in school districts that utilize a response-to-intervention (RTI) model is not successful in tiers 1 and 2 (Burns, Appleton, & Stehouwer, 2005). However, less than 2% of the student population is then referred to and placed into special education. This is an important number because current estimates of the national prevalence of learning disabilities are approximately 5–6% (Lerner, 2002).

Students in our schools may have serious academic deficits; this is a fact that no one can deny. Thus, when advocates for an RTI approach talk about preventing learning disabilities they are simply proposing that the intense needs of some children can be met without requiring a *learning disabled* (LD) label, which is important because labeling a child with a disability can negatively affect teacher expectations for them (Thelen, Burns, & Christenson, 2004) and their own attributions for success and failure (Burns, 2002). Remember, RTI is about student success, not finding children who are "truly LD."

Enhancing student success in tier 3 is dependent on a systematic problem-solving process. Students who continue to exhibit a dual discrepancy in tier 2 are then referred to the school's problem-solving team (PST) to collect more data and generate individual interventions. The process is not efficient, but should be effective if properly implemented. Yet it is often not consistently implemented (Burns, Vanderwood, & Ruby, 2005) and viewed with confusion among practitioners. The confusion may be the result of a misunderstanding of the goal. PSTs are not the keepers of a "silver bullet" intervention because such a thing does not exist, but they do know the steps needed to find the effective intervention for an individual student. Chapter 4 discussed components of an effective PST; this chapter will discuss the problem-solving process and in-depth problem analysis used by PSTs.

THE PROBLEM-SOLVING PROCESS

Bollman, Silberglitt, and Gibbons (2007) outline a five-step problem-solving process used by schools within the St. Croix River Education District (SCRED) in Minnesota buildings. The SCRED did not develop this model and was not the first to use it (Batsche & Knoff, 1995; Knoff, 2002), but the model has been effectively and consistently implemented in each SCRED school and has been a critical component of RTI. Each step in the PST process involves answering explicit questions. The steps and questions are as follows:

1. *Problem identification.* What is the discrepancy between what is expected and what is occurring?
2. *Problem analysis.* Why is the problem occurring?
3. *Developing a hypothesis.* What are the student's needs?
4. *Plan development.* What is the goal? What is the intervention plan to meet this goal? How will progress be monitored?
5. *Plan implementation.* How will intervention integrity be ensured?
6. *Plan evaluation.* Was the intervention plan successful?

Using a systematic problem-solving process differentiates PSTs from many traditional student support teams. Typically, support teams listen to the concerns of the classroom teacher and/or parent and then immediately jump to brainstorming intervention ideas. We believe that teams need a decision-making framework as they work toward developing interventions and evaluating the effects of these interventions. In the following sections, each step of the problem-solving model is described along with the task that the PST must complete at each step. Following each section is a checklist for teams to use to ensure that all steps are incorporated into the team process.

Problem Identification

The first task for the PST is to identify the problem. This step helps the team consider a variety of data to prioritize areas of concern for referred students. *Problems* are defined as a discrepancy between what is expected and what is occurring in a particular environment. It is important to remember that problems affecting student performance do not exist exclusively within the learner but may occur as the result of an interaction between learner characteristics and the demands of the educational setting. Teams should *review* information, *interview* relevant sources of information, *observe* students in a variety of settings, and *test* the student when appropriate; this series of steps bears the acronym RIOT.

In addition to sources of data, teams should consider these RIOT data in the context of *instructional, curricular, environmental,* and *learner* (ICEL) domains. For example, consider a grade 2 student reading 30 words correctly per minute in the spring. The team will compare the student's current level of performance—30 words read correctly (WRC)—to the expected level of performance (90 WRC) and conclude that the student's actual performance is below target and discrepant from local expectations, so the process should continue. Additional data are then collected to find converging evidence across multiple data points because important decisions about students should never be made on any single point of data. Additional data that may be collected in this example might include an interview with the teacher regarding in-class performance of the student or a review of past assessment data in reading. Other observations or "informal" testing with the student (e.g., curriculum-based assessment for instructional design to determine if the material represents an instructional level or nonsense word fluency to assess phonics skills) may also occur at this stage.

A second outcome of problem identification is the definition of the prioritized problem in specific quantifiable terms using data that has technical adequacy for this purpose. For example, rather than identifying a "problem in reading," a team might identify that the grade 2 student is currently reading grade-level passages at a rate of 18 WRC per minute while the expectation for grade 2 students at that time of the year is a rate of 43 WRC per minute. Or, rather than stating that "Seth is lazy," teams might identify that Seth was late to class 15 times in a semester while the expectation is that all students report to class on time. Table 7.1 displays the activities that teams need to complete at the problem identification step.

Table 7.1   Activities within the Problem Identification Stage of the Problem-Solving Process

Problem Identification Activities	Rating	Evidence/Comments
1. Are problems defined *operationally (i.e., are they observable and measurable)?*	Yes No Unsure	
2. When multiple problems are identified, does the team *prioritize them?*	Yes No Unsure	
3. Are *replacement behaviors* identified during the problem identification stage?	Yes No Unsure	
4. Does a *team member* review records, conduct an interview, make observations, and/or conduct testing to determine the presence of discrepancies between expectations and what is occurring?	Yes No Unsure	
5. Does the team use a *general education database* to identify and define problems?	Yes No Unsure	
6. Are the data collected during the problem identification stage *displayed in a graphic or summary format?*	Yes No Unsure	
7. Are there procedures for addressing the needs of *severe problems* in a timely manner?	Yes No Unsure	

Problem Analysis

Once the team has identified the problem, the next step for the PST is to analyze the problem and develop an alterable hypothesis about why the problem is occurring. This analysis will involve information collected during problem identification and may include collecting additional data. This information will be collected through a review of student records, interviews with key stakeholders, observations of student and environment, and tests as designated by the PST. Following the analysis, a hypothesis will be generated about why the problem is occurring. The hypothesis will be used to develop interventions for students.

Developing a Hypothesis

For an intervention to be effective and robust it must focus on the specific needs of the student. It should also address the reason that the student is experiencing difficulty. Student difficulty is regarded as the result of a mismatch between student need and the resources that have been provided. Rather than considering a problem to be the result of inalterable student characteristics, teams are compelled to focus on changes that can be made to the instruction, curriculum, or environment that would result in positive student outcome. The hypothesis and intervention should focus on those variables that are alterable within the school setting. These alterable variables include learning goals and objectives (what is to be learned), materials, time, student-to-teacher ratio, activities, and motivational strategies. For example, rather than considering a student's failure to master basic math facts to be the result of low IQ or lack of home support, a team may consider whether increasing student motivation, providing additional practice opportunities, or increasing levels of explicit instruction with immediate feedback would effectively ameliorate this problem. This is, of course, not to say that factors including low IQ or lack of home support do not exist; but it is inefficient for teams to spend time discussing factors over which they have little or no control when there are other avenues for intervention in which they can affect timely and meaningful change. A checklist of problem analysis activities is displayed in Table 7.2.

Plan Development

After a hypothesis has been developed about the cause of the problem, the next step is for the PST to develop a plan. Before teams engage in any discussion regarding possible intervention plans, the team must agree upon a specific goal, including a timeline for reaching this goal, and develop an individualized graph. Goals are derived from existing local or broader normative data, criterion referenced targets, or local professional expectation for acceptable performance (Fuchs & Shinn, 1989). Graphs are set up for students that include an "aim line" (i.e., a line on a graph that connects baseline data to the goal data point). This aim line defines the desired rate of progress for the student. Subsequent evaluation of interventions is based

Table 7.2   Activities within the Problem Analysis Stage
of the Problem-Solving Process

Problem Analysis Activities	Rating			Evidence/Comments
1. Does the team have a *systematic approach to analyzing problems?*	Yes	No	Unsure	
2. Does the team use *survey-level assessment* procedures to analyze academic problems?	Yes	No	Unsure	
3. Does the team use *functional behavioral assessment* techniques to analyze behavioral problems?	Yes	No	Unsure	
4. Does the team assess whether the identified problem is a *skill-based or a performance-based* problem?	Yes	No	Unsure	
5. Does the team *develop hypotheses* for why a problem may be occurring?	Yes	No	Unsure	
6. Are hypotheses focused on *"relevant" and "alterable" variables?*	Yes	No	Unsure	
7. Are hypotheses *specific, observable, measurable, and testable?*	Yes	No	Unsure	
8. Do the hypotheses generated during problem analysis consider all *potential factors that influence behavior/ academics* (e.g., child, curriculum/instructional, peer school/community factors)?	Yes	No	Unsure	
9. Are problem analysis data useful in *designing and implementing interventions?*	Yes	No	Unsure	
10. Does the team obtain *baseline data* before a plan is developed?	Yes	No	Unsure	
11. Is there a system for *communicating* problem analysis results *to parents and teachers?*	Yes	No	Unsure	

Table 7.2 (continued)   Activities within the Problem Analysis Stage of the Problem-Solving Process

Problem Analysis Activities	Rating	Evidence/Comments
12. Is there a commitment to collecting problem analysis data within 10 days of an initial referral?	Yes No Unsure	

in large part on the extent to which student progress data follow this aim line (see chapter 3).

Once the goal has been defined, the team moves on within the plan development step to create the specific intervention plan for the student. The team works to answer a number of logistical questions:

What is the intervention?
Who will implement the intervention?
Where will the intervention occur?
When will the intervention occur?
How often will the intervention occur?

Tier 3 may include a more *standardized* intervention in the purest sense of the word. For example, the Orton-Gillingham reading intervention is a fairly standardized approach for children with poor phonological skills, but it may be appropriate in tier 3 because it is an intense intervention. Empirical documentation exists to support the likely effectiveness of many standard intervention programs, even for children with severe difficulties (Kovaleski, 2003; Torgesen et al., 2001). Often the materials needed are already developed, and require little to no preparation time on the part of the interventionist. Districts can provide standard training on these interventions so that multiple staff members are prepared to implement them with students. However, in all PST instances, intervention plans are clearly defined in written form, including explicit instructions on the duration, frequency, location, materials, participants, and individual steps of the intervention. This information is recorded in "script" format such that any person could pick up the intervention plan and follow the steps, and such that an observer could view the intervention, read along on the script, and check off *yes* or *no* to the presence of each step of implementation.

The third part of the plan development step is the determination of a progress-monitoring plan. Teams utilize the same
data collection mechanism that was used to set the goal and
agree upon a frequency for assessment, as well as who will
collect the data and when it will be collected (L. S. Fuchs,
1989). Students involved in problem solving are most often
monitored weekly toward their goals. This rate of data collection allows a sufficient number of data points to be collected
in a timely manner for decision making. Table 7.3 displays the
activities to be conducted at the plan development stage.

Table 7.3   Activities within the Plan Development Stage
of the Problem-Solving Process

Plan Development Activities	Rating	Evidence/Comments
1. Is the intervention plan *supported by research*?	Yes No Unsure	
2. Is the plan a result of the problem identification and analysis processes (i.e., is the *intervention linked to the assessment*)?	Yes No Unsure	
3. Is the intervention plan *realistic to implement*?	Yes No Unsure	
4. Is the plan focused on those *factors that are most alterable* (i.e., instruction, curriculum, environment)?	Yes No Unsure	
5. Does the team *identify the goal* of an intervention plan in observable terms?	Yes No Unsure	
6. Does the intervention plan include a *description of the intervention* plan (who, what, where, when) and is it provided to all team members?	Yes No Unsure	
7. Does the intervention plan have *predetermined criteria* for evaluating its efficacy and rules for making decisions?	Yes No Unsure	

Table 7.3 (continued)   Activities within the Plan Development Stage of the Problem-Solving Process

Plan Development Activities	Rating	Evidence/Comments
8. Are the *criteria for effectiveness* attainable and realistic?	Yes No Unsure	
9. Is there a system in place to *frequently collect data* to determine if the plan is working?	Yes No Unsure	
10. Can data collected to evaluate the plan be *displayed in a graphic format?*	Yes No Unsure	
11. Is there a *commitment to continue an intervention*, as prescribed in the plan, until a team decision is made to discontinue it?	Yes No Unsure	
12. Are *parents involved* in the development of the intervention plan?	Yes No Unsure	
13. Is the *student involved* in the development of an intervention plan, when applicable?	Yes No Unsure	
14. Is there a system in place to *communicate the ongoing results* of the intervention plan with teachers and parents?	Yes No Unsure	

Plan Implementation

After teams have developed an intervention plan, the next step is to implement the plan and determine if the intervention is being implemented with integrity. Plan implementation is often an overlooked phase of many traditional intervention teams (Upah & Tilly, 2002), yet difficulty with implementation integrity is a common cause for low rates of student success (Noell, Gresham, & Gansle, 2002). For example, an intervention designed for 30 minutes per day may only actually occur for 20 minutes on 3 or 4 days out of each week due to scheduling difficulty or student absence. Moreover, the interventionist may inadvertently omit a step in the intervention that affects student performance. At the very least, if a team has defined a specific intervention to be delivered to a student, and the intervention that was actually delivered was in some way different from the plan, then success or lack thereof cannot be attributed to the original plan. We encourage schools to conduct a direct observation of all interventions in action. Observers may be other members from the PST who utilize a copy of the intervention script to document implementation integrity. Although this step may be construed as a time-intensive process due to advanced planning and scheduling, the effort is strongly warranted given the significance of potential decisions being made for students as a result of their reaction to the intervention. Schools may use the RTI process as part of the evaluation process for special education entitlement. Ethical practice standards should insist that teams make concerted efforts to ensure that lack of student progress is in no way caused by a lack of intervention integrity. Table 7.4 displays a checklist of activities for teams to conduct at the plan implementation step.

Plan Evaluation

During the final step, plan evaluation, teams review student data and make a determination regarding the success of the plan. Data gathered during the problem-solving process are used to make decisions regarding the best education strategy for a student. These decisions are based on a trend of student performance over time, during the application of the intervention, rather than on any one measure of student performance.

The major question addressed at this step is to determine whether the identified problem continues to exist. Teams will examine the data to determine if a performance discrepancy exists between what is expected and what is occurring. Data-based decisions about program evaluation can follow the decision-making guidelines discussed in chapter 3.

Specifically, in reviewing the data, teams determine if the current discrepancy between what is expected and what is occurring for a student is lesser, the same as, or greater than the original discrepancy that was identified at the start of the process. The team then determines the next steps to take. Teams may consider how to fade an intervention for a student who has experienced success or how to continue an intervention for a student who is making excellent progress but who has not yet

Table 7.4 Activities within the Plan Implementation Stage of the Problem-Solving Process

Plan Implementation Activities	Rating	Evidence/Comments
1. Does a member of the team commit to evaluating whether the intervention is being *implemented as planned?*	Yes No Unsure	
2. Is there a procedure for providing the teacher with support *if the plan is not being implemented as described?*	Yes No Unsure	
3. Is student progress toward the identified goal being evaluated on a *regular basis*, as described?	Yes No Unsure	
4. Are the data being *displayed in a graph* for decision-making purposes?	Yes No Unsure	
5. Is plan *progress communicated* with teachers and parents?	Yes No Unsure	
6. Is there *sufficient support* provided to implement intervention plans?	Yes No Unsure	
7. Are *parents involved* in implementing intervention plans?	Yes No Unsure	

met grade-level expectations. Alternately, for plans that have not been effective, teams may review data to determine if the original hypothesis concerning the cause of the problem was not accurate and if a different hypothesis better accounts for the problem. Or, teams may feel that the hypothesis is correct but that the specific intervention plan would be more successful if alterations were made for that student. Teams cycle back through this five-step process as many times as necessary to meet student needs. It is important to note that the problem-solving process is used for students receiving both general and special education services, and entitlement decisions do not change the theoretical model or practical activities of teams working toward student success. A checklist of team activities for the plan evaluation step is included in Table 7.5.

As has been stated in chapter 4, fidelity of the problem-solving process is important to a successful RTI initiative. The

Table 7.5 Activities within the Plan Evaluation Stage of the Problem-Solving Process

Plan Evaluation Activities	Rating	Evidence/Comments
1. Does the team follow *decision-making rules* when evaluating plans?	Yes No Unsure	
2. Are the baseline and progress monitoring data *displayed in a graph* for the purpose of evaluating the plan effectiveness?	Yes No Unsure	
3. Is there an agreed-upon *timeline* for plan evaluating?	Yes No Unsure	
4. When a plan has not been successful, does the team *recycle through* the problem-solving process?	Yes No Unsure	
5. When a plan is effective, are decisions made about *fading the intervention*?	Yes No Unsure	
6. Are there criteria for determining when a child's needs exceed the resources of the problem-solving team and special education *eligibility is considered*?	Yes No Unsure	

SCRED uses a case review protocol (see Table 7.6) to document that the entire problem-solving process has been followed. The case review protocol is included on the accompanying CD.

INTERVENTIONS TO USE

Once hypotheses are generated, interventions can then be developed for the hypothesized cause of the problem. As is the case with interventions in tier 2 (chapter 6), multiple interventions may be effective if they are correctly targeted. Thus, it is often necessary to implement more than one intervention to identify the causal relationship and subsequent effective approach. However, using an instructional hierarchy (Haring & Eaton, 1978) may help efficiently identify learner characteristics that can lead to alterable hypotheses. Chapter 3

Table 7.6 Case Review Protocol for Problem-Solving Analysis

Standard	Intervention 1	Intervention 2
Problem Identification		
■ An initial discrepancy has been defined in observable measurable terms and is quantified.		
■ Documented data from at least two sources converge to support the discrepancy statement.		
■ Student baseline data in the area of concern has been collected using a measurement system with sufficient technical adequacy for ongoing frequent measurement, and includes a minimum of 3 data points with standardized procedures for assessment. Baseline data have been graphed.		
Problem Analysis		
■ Data from a variety of sources (RIOT) and domains (ICEL) have been collected to consider multiple hypotheses for the cause of the identified discrepancy. These data have been documented.		
■ A single hypothesis for the cause of the discrepancy has been selected. At least two pieces of data converge to support this hypothesis. At least one of these is quantitative.	■	■
Problem Development		
■ A data-based goal has been established that describes the learner, conditions (time and materials for responding), expected performance, and a goal date. The goal has been indicated on a graph.	■	■
■ The intervention selected meets federal definitions of scientifically research-based intervention. The selected intervention directly addresses the specific identified problem and the hypothesis for the cause of the discrepancy.	■	■
■ A written intervention plan has been clearly defined that explicitly describes what will be done, where, when, how often, how long (per session), by whom, and with what resources.	■	■
■ A written description of the progress-monitoring plan has been completed and includes who will collect data, data collection methods, conditions for data collections, and schedule.	■	■
■ A decision-making rule has been selected for use.	■	■
■ A plan evaluation meeting has been set for no more than 8 weeks after the plan is established.	■	■

Table 7.6 (continued) Case Review Protocol for Problem-Solving Analysis		
Standard	Intervention 1	Intervention 2
Problem Implementation		
■ A direct observation of the intervention has been completed at least one time. Any discrepancies between the written plan and the intervention in action have been noted and resolved. Observations have been continued until the intervention being delivered and the written intervention plan match. Written documentation of each observation has been made.	■	■
■ Data have been collected and graphed as stated in the plan. The required number of data points have been collected under the same intervention conditions after the establishment of integrity.	■	■
Problem Evaluation		
■ The team has documented agreement that the plan was carried out as intended.	■	■
■ The team has determined and documented whether the pre-intervention discrepancy decreased, increased, or stayed the same during the plan implementation phase.	■	■
■ The team has decided to continue the plan unmodified, to develop a modified plan, to fade the plan, or to terminate the plan. The team has documented this decision.	■	■

discussed how to identify the phase in which the student is performing; Table 7.7 lists interventions appropriate for each phase. A common example of the importance of matching instruction/intervention to learning phase is a math minute (sometimes called a *mad minute*) in which an entire class completes a sheet of randomly selected math facts (e.g., single-digit multiplication) for 1 or 2 minutes and each student tries to improve on her most recent score. This is a potentially strong instructional support if the student has learned math facts with high accuracy but is working on getting faster at them (the proficiency phase). If the child is already proficient, then this is a waste of instructional time, albeit a short one, and the data may be helpful. If the student is in the acquisition phase, then she may practice facts incorrectly and learn inaccurate answers to automaticity. Thus, she would have to unlearn the incorrect fact in order to learn the correct one. It is likely that most of the students would be in the proficiency phase shortly

Table 7.7 Interventions for Students Based on Instructional Hierarchy

Phase	Acquisition	Proficiency	Generalization	Adaptation
General Principle	Learning is inaccurate and slow. Focus is on initial learning of the concept/fact.	Learning is accurate but slow. Focus is on increasing the speed of task completion.	Learning is proficient, and can be applied to different settings and stimuli. Focus is applying the task to novel settings and applications.	Learning is proficient and can be applied to solve problems. Focus is on generating solutions to challenges.
Interventions	Modeling and close performance monitoring with immediate feedback and error correction (e.g., listening passage preview, incremental rehearsal, choral responding, discrimination trials, math manipulatives).	High repetition in the new task with brief feedback (e.g., repeated reading, math minute, timed readings, overcorrection).	Provide independent practice with different settings and delayed feedback. Here is where homework can be assigned (e.g., learning centers).	Provide challenging situations and teach core elements of technique and how to apply them (e.g., simulations, thinking games).

after introducing the fact, but for those who are not the intervention could actually do more harm than good.

In addition to being correctly targeted, the intervention should include explicit instruction of the deficit skill and high opportunities to respond, and should provide an appropriate level of challenge with appropriate feedback (Burns, VanDer-Heyden, & Boice, in press). Thus, when selecting from the entire universe of potential intervention strategies, all of which claim to be research based, interventions should consider if these criteria exist and select interventionists that are consistent with these guiding principles. However, not all interventions are guided toward the learner. For example, if a student can only correctly read 85% of the words within the learning material from the given reading curriculum, which represents the frustration level (see chapter 3), then the intervention may very well be the use of different curricular material.

BRIEF EXPERIMENTAL ANALYSIS

Even after identifying the specific deficit skill and the phase of student functioning, there may still be different reasons why the student is experiencing difficulties. Daly, Witt, Martens, and Dool (1997) have proposed five hypotheses for student difficulty including: (1) the child does not want to do the task; (2) the child has not practiced enough; (3) the child has not had enough help with the task; (4) the child is being asked to complete the task in a way he never has before; and (5) the task is too difficult. These then can become a system of hypothesis testing within a brief experimental analysis (BEA) in which the interventionist quickly tests the relative effects of two or more interventions on the target behavior. BEA seems to have a great deal of potential for identifying interventions within an RTI framework for children with the most severe difficulties (Barnett, Daly, Jones, & Lentz, 2004).

BEA is based on the assumption that changes in instructional variables can affect immediate academic performance (Daly et al., 1997). Thus, instructional variables are manipulated by implementing a series of interventions and assessing the immediate affect on reading fluency within one passage. For example, an interventionist would start by having the student read one grade-level passage to establish a baseline. The interventionist would then test the first hypothesis for failure by offering a reinforcer if the student improves his score by

30%. If the fluency score increases by a predetermined criterion (e.g., an increase of 30 WRC per minute, or a 70% increase over baseline; Burns & Wagner, 2007), then the first hypothesis is confirmed and a motivation intervention is designed. If not, the next hypotheses are quickly tested in a similar fashion using repeated reading for the second hypothesis, listening passage preview or phrase drill for the third, and easier material for the fifth. The fourth hypothesis is usually not tested within the BEA because it addresses how the task is assigned and assessed during learning. Commonly used interventions within BEA are presented in Table 7.8, along with descriptions of each.

Data are obtained for each hypothesis, and the two interventions that led to the largest gain are repeated in reverse order with a different set of reading stimuli. Data from a sample BEA is displayed in Figure 7.1. This sample finds that phrase drill and easier material lead to greater increases over baseline than do other interventions. After returning to the baseline, the two interventions are again compared and easier material leads to the larger gain. Thus, for this student it could be hypothesized that the reason for failure is that the material is too difficult and easier curricular material should be used as the intervention.

Table 7.8 Glossary of Common Interventions Used in Brief Experimental Analysis

Intervention	Definition
Incentive	The interventionist provides a positively reinforcing item or privilege to the student if she meets an oral reading fluency goal such as increase over baseline by 30%.
Student passage preview	The student reads the passage silently and asks the interventionist to read aloud unfamiliar words.
Listening passage preview	The interventionist reads the passage aloud while the student follows along on a different copy of the passage and points to each word as it is read.
Repeated reading	The student reads the same passage aloud three or four times for 2 or 3 minutes each time, with no corrective feedback.
Phrase drill	After the student reads the passage, the interventionist points to each word that the student misreads and tells the student the word. The student then reads the word in isolation, after which he rereads the phrase or sentence at least three times.

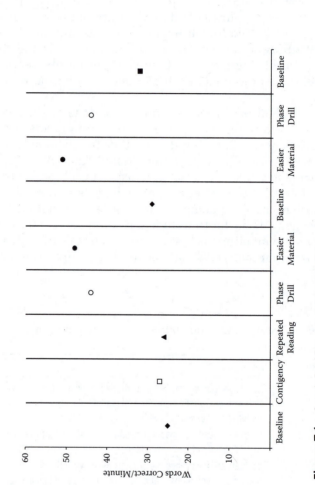

Figure 7.1   Sample Brief Experimental Analysis Data.

CONCLUSION

Tier 3 is like tier 2 in many ways. For example, both involve attempting interventions, using some level of problem solving, frequent monitoring of student progress, and focusing on student learning. However, tier 3 interventions are for students whose needs warrant more intensive approaches derived from an in-depth problem-solving process. Thus, the core components of tier 3 are the use of a PST to generate hypotheses about student difficulties from a variety of data. PSTs are often inconsistently implemented and dismissed as ineffective, but adherence to core problem-solving principles can result in immediate and dramatic changes in student behavior.

8

Frequently Asked Questions Regarding Implementation and Tips for Getting Started

The purpose of this chapter is to review commonly asked questions about response-to-intervention (RTI) implementation and discuss tips for getting started and sustaining implementation. As part of the RTI implementation process, teachers employed by Minnesota's St. Croix River Education District (SCRED) member districts attend quarterly RTI forums to ask questions and give input about the process. Many of the questions and answers from these SCRED forums are presented in this chapter. Grateful credit is given here to the SCRED RTI Workgroup (Kerry Bollman, Kim Gibbons, Chris McHugh, Jeff Menigo, Barb Scierka, and Ben Silberglitt) for the answers to these questions.

FREQUENTLY ASKED QUESTIONS

Roles, Responsibilities and Intervention Standards

Who Is Responsible for Implementing the Intervention and for Collecting Data?

We suggest that the responsibility for developing interventions is assigned at the creation of the problem-solving team (PST). Typically, a member of the PST will consult with the regular classroom teacher and assist in designing an intervention. In most cases, regular education resources are used to deliver the intervention. Special education resources may be used for data collection to evaluate intervention effectiveness. It should be noted that there is language in the Individuals with Disabilities Education Act (IDEA) that allows for incidental benefit to regular education students. This means that in some cases, regular education students may receive instruction from a special education teacher if their needs are similar to those of other students in the instructional group.

What Is the Role of the Special Education Teacher on the Problem-Solving Team?

The special education teacher should be one of the academic specialists on the PST. As such, the special education teacher may assist in conducting assessment to design an appropriate intervention (reviewing information, interviewing, observing, conducting diagnostic testing) and in evaluating whether the intervention is effective.

How Do Teams Apply Interventions in the Secondary Setting and Who Is Responsible?

The academic specialist on the PST assists with this task and works to identify intervention resources (peer tutoring, general education classes with extra support, help during study hall, etc.). The team needs to determine the nature of the intervention and at what level of rigor it is designed. School principals are encouraged to offer an array of services within a multitiered model to support students.

How Do Teams Identify Scientifically Research-Based Interventions?

Teams are encouraged to use interventions that meet the federal guidelines of scientifically research-based (SRB) interventions. SRB interventions are those that involve the application of rigorous systematic and objective procedures to obtain reliable and valid knowledge relevant to education activities and programs. In addition, SRB interventions involve research that employs systematic, empirical methods that draw on observation or experiment, and rigorous data analyses that are adequate to test the stated hypotheses and justify the general conclusions drawn.

What Constitutes a Rigorous Intervention?

When determining whether an intervention is rigorous, there are two factors to consider. First, the team must ask whether enough time is allocated to deliver the intervention. Most powerful interventions are delivered at least 4 to 5 days per week for a sufficient amount of time (enough time to complete the program). Second, the team must consider whether the intervention is scientifically based. If the amount of time allocated to the intervention is insufficient and the intervention is not supported through empirical research, then the PST needs to discuss why it thinks the intervention is "rigorous." Although no empirical research exists to provide a single standard for rigor across all interventions, suggestions of 30 minutes of additional time in small groups (those of four to six students) for 3 to 5 days per week using empirically supported materials have been made by researchers and consultants in the field.

Who Is Responsible for Determining Whether an Intervention Is Rigorous?

Determining whether an intervention is rigorous enough is a decision made by the PST. The PST is responsible for ensuring that the intervention is clearly defined, that the interventionist is appropriately trained, and that intervention integrity occurs. If it is determined that the intervention is not being delivered as designed, more support should be provided to the interventionist.

Treatment Integrity

How Is Treatment Integrity Verified?

Treatment integrity should be verified through multiple approaches that include direct observations. The PST should determine which member of the team will conduct a direct observation of the intervention. Any member of the PST may complete observations, and teams are encouraged to make full use of all resources on the team rather than assigning all observations to a single team member. Someone outside of the PST could serve as observer if she is familiar with the intervention. Teams should plan for the observation in advance. In addition to observations, permanent product and completed procedural checklists may assist in assessing treatment and PST integrity.

Is It Necessary to Verify Treatment Integrity?

We have observed that some teams struggle to find time to do these checks, and some teachers feel that *they themselves*—rather than the plan—are being evaluated. An intervention needs to be implemented as planned in order to determine if it is effective. If the intervention is not implemented as designed, progress (or lack thereof) cannot be attributed to the specific intervention plan. As a result, response-to-intervention cannot be determined. The purpose of the implementation integrity check is to support the interventionist through assessing whether the written intervention plan is logistically feasible, whether needed materials are available, and whether the implementer is finding the written procedures usable under current conditions. In situations in which the written plan and the performed intervention do not match, teams must choose to alter one or the other to make them match. The integrity check is not meant to be evaluative of the intervention implementer personally; rather, it is an important service to the student to certify that meaningful, data-based decision making on the student's behalf may continue. Integrity checks also provide a protection to the implementer and the team. If an intervention is not successful and integrity is questioned, the implementer has more than his "word" that the intervention was fully implemented as planned. The implementation integrity check should take place within a few days of the implementation start date to ensure that valuable time is not lost on implementing an intervention that is different from the plan or on implementing an intervention as written when it is found to be practically ineffectual. Within a system in which we will potentially label a child as being disabled based on the child's response to our intervention efforts, it is critical that we make strong efforts to ensure that no part of the child's lack of response may be attributed to poor intervention design or implementation.

What Should Be Done if after the Integrity Check the Plan Is Not Being Implemented Properly?

A team will not want to evaluate progress based on data collected when the intervention has not been implemented as planned. Therefore, teams may draw a new intervention line on the progress monitoring graph to indicate updated intervention and evaluate data after this line. This is a good reason to check integrity early!

Interventions and Student Progress

For Those Students Who Demonstrate Continued Need for Supportive Interventions but Make Progress Given These Supports Such That They Don't Qualify to Receive Special Education Services, Do We Continue General Education Interventions Forever?

Yes. We would expect that up to 20% of students in our schools will need additional support on an ongoing basis to make adequate progress. The majority of these students are not labeled with a special education disability. However, special education should be considered if the services needed for success are too resource intensive to continue without special education eligibility.

What Is the Best Way to Fade out Interventions When a Student Has Made Successful Progress?

Teams could consider fading interventions when students have 3–5 *consecutive* data points at or above the "aim line" or when the performance score meets the predetermined criterion. (Please see chapters 2 and 3.)

Measurement

How Should Teams Determine What Level of Instructional Material to Use for Progress Monitoring?

In most instances, students should be monitored with grade-level material. In instances in which the student reads less than 10 words correctly per minute on grade-level probes, survey-level assessment procedures may be used to work backward to find the highest grade level of probe at which the student reads at least 10 words correctly per minute and use that level of probe for progress monitoring. If the amount of growth to reach the spring season target score from the student's current baseline score would represent an unrealistically aggressive goal, teams should use a two-word-per-week growth rate to set goals within tier 3. Special education entitlement decisions must be made on the basis of student performance (level and slope) on grade-level materials.

How Often Should Data Be Collected and over What Period of Time?

Data collection should match the severity of the problem. Thus, students in tier 3 should be monitored weekly until enough data points are gathered to obtain a reliable slope. Students in tier 2 interventions may be monitored biweekly or even monthly.

When Calculating Slope, Should Data for the Whole School Year Be Used, or Just Data after the Implementation of the Intervention?

Teams are encouraged to obtain 8–10 data points per intervention. However, if a decision is made to change interventions before 8–10 data points are obtained, the team can combine data across intervention periods. Teams should not use data collected prior to an intervention to calculate slope. For example, consider the student who had benchmark data collected in September and progress monitoring data collected in October and November. The student was brought to the attention of the PST in mid-November and an intervention was developed and implemented on November 30. The team should only use data collected after November 30 to calculate slope.

How Much Baseline Data Should Be Collected to Set up a Graph?

When collecting baseline data to graph for academic assessments, always collect at least three samples and take the median score.

Special Education Entitlement

At What Point Does RTI Documentation Start?

Documentation starts when a student is identified for a tier 2 intervention. If the student is eventually referred for special education eligibility evaluation, then the mandated timeline starts when the parent gives consent for an evaluation. We are recommending that the evaluation not start until the team has confirmed that all necessary documentation will be fully complete prior to the end of the evaluation timeline.

For Students Who Transfer in from Another School District and Are Eligible for Learning Disabled (LD) Services under a Traditional Evaluation, How Is Eligibility Addressed?

Students who transfer in with an active individual education plan (IEP) do not need to go through the eligibility determination process if state criteria are followed. The PST can adopt the IEP and monitor its progress. Teams should review data on level and slope compared to new district expectations. If the student does not have significant instructional needs, the team can decide to end special education services or develop a reintegration plan and monitor progress for 45 days without any special education services.

Is It Fair to Identify Students as LD Based on Local Norms—That Is, Labeling Someone LD in One District but Not Another?

Yes. The current system has the same flaw; it's just hidden within the referral process. Entitlement decisions should be viewed more as an allocation of resources. Schools use special education services to serve students with the greatest needs instead of using a process to discover which student has a specific learning disability. In addition, eligibility is always a two-part question: Does the student meet the criteria for a disability, and if so, does the student have significant education needs? Thus, there may be students in one district who have instructional needs in that district but not in another.

What Are the Problems with Using a Severe Discrepancy Model to Identify Students as LD?

An abundance of research exists that documents significant problems with the use of IQ/achievement discrepancy models. Three common themes emerge when studying the research base on such models. First, the discrepancy criterion forces children to fail for several years ("wait to fail") before they can enter the special education system because discrepancies are rarely large enough for qualification until after third grade. Research and best practices indicate that early intervention is key rather than waiting until grade 3 or later, when remediation of skills becomes extremely difficult. Second, IQ/achievement discrepancy models are not valid. There is no evidence that students who have a severe discrepancy behave and can be treated in qualitatively different ways because of the discrepancy. Third, IQ tests lack treatment validity. These tests contribute little reliable information for planning, implementing, and evaluating instructional interventions (Aaron, 1997).

What Are the Advantages to Using RTI as One Factor in Identifying Students as LD?

There are many advantages to RTI. First, the "wait to fail" model is eliminated, and schools can operate under a preventative model focused on early intervention. Second, there is a clear link between assessment and intervention. Third, the emphasis in special education is shifted away from eligibility and focused toward getting students the interventions they need in order to be successful. Fourth, the model is conceptual as well as practical. Fifth, the model is multidisciplinary and increases teaming. By creating a language of skills and instruction as opposed to disability and pathology, barriers between general and special education may be removed. Sixth, school psychologists will have increased time to focus on functional assessment activities that are directly linked to intervention planning. Seventh, the model emphasizes serving students in the least restrictive environment.

Is It True That There Is Limited Research on Implementing RTI on a Large Scale?

Any time new educational practices are "brought to scale," challenges exist with moving from policy to implementation. Technical assistance will need to be provided to districts on progress monitoring techniques, intervention development, and intervention implementation. However, several studies have been conducted examining interventions for students with learning and/or behavioral problems that included RTI as a component (Heartland Area Education Agency 11, 2004; Kovaleski, Gickling, & Morrow, 1998; Marston, Muyskens, Lau, & Canter, 2003; McNamara & Hollinger, 2003). Moreover, descriptions of many large-scale implementation efforts are available in the literature (Jimerson, Burns, & VanDerHeyden, 2007). While it may seem that resources are inadequate for the implementation of RTI, the real challenge is to use existing resources to improve student outcomes through better educational practices. In the area of LD, much emphasis has been placed on regulatory compliance, and many states have been apprehensive about doing anything that deviates from current IDEA mandates. Although there are questions about implementation of RTI approaches, they do not undermine the reasons for looking to more effective models for instruction and intervention (Gresham, 2002). Four consensus reports at the national level have concluded that the research base on RTI is sound. The true benefits of changed practices need to be evaluated over time. There is consensus that the evidence is sufficient to justify large-scale implementation of RTI at this time (Bradley, Danielson, & Hallahan, 2002; Donovan & Cross, 2002; Finn, Rotherham, & Hokansen, 2001; President's Commission on Excellence in Special Education, 2001).

How Do We Know We Are Identifying the Right Students?

Finding the "right" students is not the most pressing educational challenge for special education. It is shameful to provide regulations that seem to force our schools to continue to engage in practices for which there is little evidence of either prevention or effective intervention. As Fletcher et al. note, "Our most pressing challenge is conveying urgency about preventing disabilities through early screening and effective instruction, and, for those who do not respond sufficiently, providing effective special education interventions that change achievement and social/behavioral outcomes" (In press, p. 11). A lengthy body of evidence has suggested that schools serve students with the most severe achievement deficits compared to other students in their own communities even when encumbered by the ability-achievement discrepancy mode (Deno, Marston, Shinn, & Tindal, 1983; Peterson & Shinn, 2002; Shinn & Marston, 1985; Shinn, Tindal & Spira, 1987; Shinn, Tindal, & Stein, 1988; Shinn, Ysseldyke, Deno, & Tindal, 1986). Schools have been finding the "right" students; it is just that too many of them are finally identified too late; the methods are time consuming, not directly related to treatment, consume valuable intervention resources, and often require schools to ignore all the data they have collected because they don't match the students' unmet severe educational needs.

Won't We Overidentify Students as LD Using an RTI Approach?

Data from other states and districts using an RTI approach do not indicate that students are overidentified as LD. In fact, meta-analytic research has found that districts that use RTI identify less than 2% of the students as LD, which compares to the national average of about 5%. Data collected from the SCRED over the past 11 years has shown a 50% reduction in the number of students identified as LD. At the same time, major gains in achievement for all students have been demonstrated.

Other Areas

How Does RTI Apply to the Area of Behavior?

RTI is the practice of providing high-quality instruction and interventions matched to student need, monitoring progress frequently to make changes in instruction, and applying child response data to important educational decisions. The process is equally useful for academic or behavioral issues. Positive behavior support (PBS) also uses a three-tiered model of intervention and data-based decision making. In fact, RTI is an extension of the same theory from which PBS derives.

Is the RTI Process Appropriate for English Language Learners?

Yes. Many districts with large English language learner (ELL) populations use the RTI process as a way to conduct

nondiscriminatory assessment and to verify the effectiveness of interventions. Part of the assessment within RTI for
ELLs involves assessments of English proficiency and reading
skills in the student's native language. Those data are then
used to help determine interventions. Moreover, one category
of difficulties for which tier 2 interventions are implemented
could include ELL instruction. Although research is currently
underway to examine the effectiveness of RTI for students who
are ELLs, previous studies have suggested that these students
experience enhanced learning as well at a rate that is often not
consistent with proficiency in the English language (Healy,
Vanderwood, & Edelston, 2005; Vanderwood & Nam, 2007).

IMPLEMENTATION TIPS

How to Start the Process

Implementation of an RTI system is not something that happens overnight! Districts are encouraged to conduct a needs
assessment of the three main elements of RTI (measurement,
instruction, and the problem-solving model) and begin implementation slowly over 4 or 5 years. A sample RTI needs a

checklist and a district level planning questionnaire is
included on the accompanying CD. To expect long-term implementation, strong support at the state and district leadership
level is necessary. Training and support must ensure that practice and feedback are available to districts in sufficient quantity. Prior to implementation, districts must obtain "buy-in"
from all key stakeholders including superintendents, principals, curriculum directors, teachers, and parents. Districts
starting from "scratch" may consider the following 4-year
phase-in process:

Sample Four-Year Phase-in Process

Year One Activities

Build awareness with key stakeholders about the inter-
face between the No Child Left Behind Act and the
IDEA.

Build awareness with key stakeholders about RTI and
related concepts.

Establish and implement a schoolwide measurement system. Conduct benchmark assessment of all students
three times per year and progress monitoring for students below target.

Provide training to teams on general outcome measurement, preparing to do schoolwide assessment, interpreting benchmark data, goal setting, graphing, and decision-making rules.

Provide a "coach" to assist with helping the school prepare for benchmark assessment, interpreting reports and data utilization, and trouble-shooting problems.

Year 2 Activities

Provide staff development opportunities for teachers on implementing an effective beginning reading curriculum.

Identify supplemental interventions and provide training.

Provide staff development opportunities on using a standardized framework for evaluating curriculum.

Provide a coach to evaluate the fidelity of curriculum and instructional strategy implementation.

Continue implementing the measurement system with coaching.

Identify and/or establish a problem-solving team in each school to participate in Year 3 training.

Identify problem-solving team facilitators to attend training on the problem-solving model with a focus on academic difficulties.

Year 3 Activities

Begin tier 2 intervention.

Provide training to problem-solving teams on the problem-solving model.

Provide coaching for problem-solving teams.

Continue implementing the measurement system with coaching as needed.

Continue providing coaching on curriculum and instructional strategy implementation.

Determine eligibility procedures for Year 4.

Year 4 Activities

Continue implementing the measurement system with coaching as needed.

Problem-solving teams should meet regularly with a coaching component for entitlement decisions.

Consider networking meetings where problem-solving team facilitators and coaches attend monthly networking meetings.

Lessons Learned about RTI Implementation

Implementation of an RTI model at the SCRED has resulted in many "lessons learned" over the past few years. The top 10 lessons learned are described here.

Lesson 1: A multitiered service delivery model is critical. RTI implementation is predicated on the notion that a continuum of service delivery options is available in each school. In schools where special education services are the only way of providing help to students, large numbers of special education referrals can be expected. Developing a multitiered model requires efficient use of resources and a great deal of instructional "teaming."

Lesson 2: Principals are key players. As instructional leaders in their own school buildings, it is imperative to involve principals early and often in the RTI planning and implementation process. Principals should be active participants on the problem-solving team to assist in providing support and resources for at-risk students.

Lesson 3: Ongoing training and support is critical. To sustain RTI implementation, districts are advised to build in an active "coaching" component to assist staff in skill development. Ongoing training should be provided to grade-level teams and problem-solving teams on data-based decision making and research-based interventions. Districts are advised to identify an in-district expert "troubleshooter" to assist schools with RTI implementation.

Lesson 4: Teach patience and flexibility. RTI implementation is a work in progress. It is important that all key stakeholders recognize that the system needs to be evaluated regularly and medications and adjustments made accordingly. Decisions cannot be made in a "top down" manner. All key stakeholders need to work together to implement the process and address questions.

Lesson 5: Documentation of the process is critical. While RTI is primarily about system reform of regular education, there is a special education entitlement component. Accordingly, schools must have a clearly defined problem-solving process with forms and guidelines to guide the process. The SCRED has found that even with intensive oversight of the process, problems with documentation still existed.

Lesson 6: Intervention integrity is a hot issue and should not be ignored. Within an RTI model, it is critical to evaluate whether interventions are implemented as designed. It is important to highlight that this process is meant to be supportive rather than evaluative. Schools are encouraged to discuss in advance a process for determining which team members will conduct integrity observations.

Lesson 7: The standard treatment protocol approach has its place. We recommend that districts examine benchmark data and design standard treatment protocol interventions for groups of students as a starting point. If students do not make progress with the standard treatment protocol intervention, then problem-solving teams can customize individual interventions using the problem-solving process. Teams can become easily overwhelmed if they try to individualize interventions for all students rather than start with group-level interventions.

Lesson 8: Expect questions and occasional conflict. Any time a system is undergoing change, conflict should be expected. It is important to keep your "eye on the prize" and emphasize that while change may be difficult for adults, RTI works for students!

Lesson 9: Schools weak on one or more of the core RTI areas will struggle. We found that the problem-solving teams that struggled the most were from schools that did not have a multitiered service delivery model and a lack of organization at the grade level (i.e., lack of regular grade-level team meetings). It is always important to examine data and determine if an achievement problem is a system problem or an individual student problem.

Lesson 10: Avoid entitlement decisions until core RTI features are in place! Districts will have great difficulty making entitlement decisions if all elements of RTI are not in place. For example, if a formative assessment system is not in place, districts will be unable to assess a student's rate of progress. If problem-solving teams do not use a systematic decision-making model, interventions will not be individualized. And, if the team does not use scientific, research-based interventions, student progress is likely to be minimal.

CONCLUSION

There are decades of examples of school districts implementing an innovation with great enthusiasm at the beginning, but then abandoning the approach later when difficulties arise. If we are not careful, RTI could be the latest in the long list of programs that were "tried years ago," which would be unfortunate because RTI represents the best chance for substantive change since the Education of All Handicapped Children Act (later, the IDEA) was first passed. Issues will certainly arise as implementation occurs on a national level within individual districts. We cannot foresee every potential problem, but we can predict that problems will occur. School districts stand the best chance in overcoming implementation difficulties if they phase in RTI over time, focus on enhanced learning rather than identifying LD, focus on tiers 1 and 2 in addition to tier 3, operationally define RTI, assure implementation fidelity for the process and treatments within, and match interventions to the individual needs of students (Burns, 2007).

Perhaps more important than the preparations discussed above could very well be the mind-set of those creating and implementing them. The conversation about RTI implementation needs to continue, and we hope this book will help facilitate that conversation. Nothing stated in the pages of this volume is set in stone, which means modifications will be made either as research continues to inform practice or as individual schools find necessitated revisions based on their own unique systems. However, we must not think of RTI as something that can succeed or fail, because in order for RTI to have a positive affect on students we have to recognize it as a paradigmatic change rather than a specific tool. It is instead a commitment to data-based resource allocation and targeted interventions (Burns, 2007).

The federal provision allows local educational agencies to choose an RTI or traditional approach. We contend that this was a problematic but wise decision. There will be inconsistencies among school districts, but that inconsistency already exists in a much more masked manner. The option allows for gradual implementation based on school readiness and need, and school districts can avoid using RTI data to determine eligibility until they collect and provide data demonstrating that an RTI model is implemented with fidelity.

Finally, RTI is also a commitment to *all* children by *all* educators. They can no longer be "your kids" and "my kids"; they are *all* "our kids." We need to think of gifted students, students experiencing success in the core curriculum, *and* students who are struggling as our personal responsibilities.

RTI provides the mechanism to address the needs of all students if we commit to it. However, RTI should not be continued unless data demonstrate that all children are learning; we predict that with adherence to the principles discussed here and a willingness to evolve, they will!

Appendix A

A Short Introduction to RTI—PowerPoint Presentation

Response-To-Intervention

Linking Assessment to Intervention to
Help All Children
Matthew K. Burns, Ph.D.
University of Minnesota

**An LEA "may use a process that determines
if the child responds to scientific, research-
based intervention as a part of the evaluation
procedures" (Pub. L. No. 108–446 § 614
[b][6][A]; § 614 [b][2 & 3]).**

How did we get here?

- Accountability and proficiency
  - NCLB
- When was LD born?
  - PL 94-142–1975
  - Regulations – 1977
  - Discrepancy was a compromise (Gresham et al., 2004).
- IRLD
  - University of Minnesota (Ysseldyke & Deno)
  - Early 1980s

Interventions for Children with LD

Mnemonic strategies	1.62
Reading comprehension	1.13
Behavior modification	0.93
Direct instruction	0.84
Psycholinguistic training	0.39
Modality instruction	0.15
Diet	0.12
Perceptual training	0.08

Special Education Meta-Analyses

- $d = -0.12$
- What is special education???

Specialized instruction, at no cost
to the parents or guardians, to meet
the unique needs of a child with a
disability.

Accountability

- Reauthorization of the Elementary and Secondary Education Act

- RTI was born in special education, but it was conceived in NCLB

Table *Demographic Information*

Group	Sex	Pre	Post*	IQ	ADD?	Medication
1/D	M	13	55	103	Yes	Adderal
2/D	M	02	59	95	Yes	Ritalin
3/D	M	02	38	110	No	Ritalin
4/D	F	03	55	105	Yes	Ritalin
5/D	F	02	50	110	Yes	Ritalin
6/D	M	18	60	101	No	—
7/D	M	01	38	98	Yes	Ritalin
8/D	M	01	45	102	No	—
9/NI	M	38	39	99	No	—
10/NI	F	50	48	107	No	—
11/NI	M	85	83	122	No	—
12/NI	M	82	85	101	No	—
13/NI	M	60	60	113	No	—
14/NI	M	52	50	95	No	—
15/NI	M	49	53	99	Yes	Ritalin
16/NI	M	75	74	121	No	—

*Follow-up testing was performed using alternate forms. Simos, et al., 2001.

Group Results

- Experimental group increased 44.75 points (SD = 7.22)

- Correlation between growth and IQ

- $r = -0.29$

What is the answer????

Pine River El: Pine River – Backus
J.W. Smith: Bemidji
Sebeka El.: Sebeka
Harrison El.: Brainerd
Lincoln El.: Brainerd
Longfellow Choice: Rochester
McGregor El.: McGregor
Laura MacArthur El.: Duluth
Nettleton Magnet School: Duluth
Dayton's Bluff El.: St. Paul
Farnsworth Magnet School: St. Paul
Museum Magnet/Rondo School: St. Paul
Roosevelt Magnet School: St. Paul

Keys to Success
St. Paul Pioneer Press June 4, 2006

- Reading Above All Else
  - Emphasize reading and writing especially K-2

- Beyond the Classroom
  - After school programs and social services

- Continuous Assessment/Small-Group Instruction
  - Formal and informal assessments to provide an appropriate level of challenge

- Effective Staff
  - Strong leadership and cohesive staff with co-planning

- Structured, Disciplined Environment

An Approach to Solving Problems

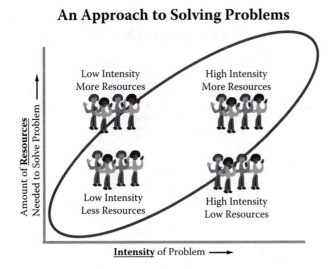

R (or R or R) – T – I (or I)

- Response or responsiveness or resistance

- T = to

- Instruction or intervention
  - Standard protocol or problem solving

Multitiered Interventions (Burns, Deno, & Jimerson, 2007)

1. General Education: Universal screening, progress monitoring, quality core curricula and instruction: All students,

2. Standard Protocol Treatments: Small group tutoring (4 to 6) in general education with at least monthly monitoring: 20% of students at any time

3. Problem Solving: Individualized interventions in with at least weekly monitoring: 5% of students at any time

Tier 2

- Effective – at least moderate effect size
- Costs – Low as possible, cost/effect size, cost effective (comes with a lot), dedicated teacher time
- Delivery
  - Group/individual (two to six considering efficiency)
  - Total students (20%)
  - Who - teacher supervision with some peer and or adult tutoring
  - Pull out – in addition to, some pull out component, 3 to 5X/week, approximately 30 minutes (kinder – 20 min tops). No less than 8 weeks.
- Grades of kids – earlier better, certainly K-2
- Measure – fluency measure of reading at least monthly
- Materials
  - Ease – much easier if compiled, but not prerequisite
  - Availability – standardized (manual)

Components of Tier 3

- Precise measurement on a frequent basis

- Individualized and intensive interventions

- Meaningful multidisciplinary collaboration regarding individual kids

Results

- More children demonstrated proficient skill levels on state accountability tests (Heartland, 2004; Sornson et al., 2005)

- Fewer children were retained in a grade (Kovaleski et al., 1995).

- Improved reading skills among children identified as at-risk (Marston et al., 2003; Tilly, 2003),

- Increased time on task, task comprehension, and task completion (Kovaleski, Gickling, & Morrow, 1999).

Special Education in RTI

- Includes more services and was more intense (Ikeda & Gustafson, 2002; Reschly & Starkweather, 1997)

- Happened at earlier grades (Reschly & Starkweather, 1997)

- Was more cost effective (Sornson et al., 2005)

- Was directly linked resources with student needs (Tilly, 2003)

What do we need to do?

- Frequent monitoring

- Data-based decision making

- Ongoing support in general education

- Multidisciplinary

Evaluation Review

- Who, what, why, and when (within 30 school days).

- What if you just didn't do it?

Appendix B

Assessment

Assessment Instruments and Cutoff Scores for Proficiency and Accuracy in Order to Target Interventions (Kindergarten to Grade 2)

Area	Kindergarten	First Grade	Second Grade
General outcome	Initial sound fluency	Letter naming fluency	Oral reading fluency
Measure	Letter naming fluency	Word list fluency	

Oral Reading Fluency

Fluency	Proficiency NA	Proficiency < 12 words/ minute	Proficiency < 25 words/ minute
	Accuracy < 93%	Accuracy < 93%	Accuracy < 93%

Nonsense Word Fluency

Phonics	Proficiency < 5 sounds/minute	Proficiency < 13 sounds/ minute	Proficiency < 30 sounds/ minute
	Accuracy < 90%	Accuracy < 90%	Accuracy < 90%

Phoneme Segmentation Fluency

Phonemic awareness	Proficiency < 7	Proficiency < 10	Proficiency < 10
	Accuracy < 90%	Accuracy < 90%	Accuracy < 90%

Sources: Proficiency cutoff scores for oral reading fluency are based on the 25th percentile from Hasbrouk and Tindall (2006); proficiency scores for nonsense words and phoneme segmentation fluency are based on Dynamic Indicators of Basic Early Literacy Skills standards for at-risk students.

Assessment Instruments and Cutoff Scores for Proficiency and Accuracy in Order to Target Interventions (Grades 3–5)

Area	Third Grade	Fourth Grade	Fifth Grade
General outcome Measure	Oral reading fluency	Oral reading fluency	Oral reading fluency
Oral Reading Fluency			
Fluency	Proficiency < 45 words/minute	Proficiency < 69 words/ minute	Proficiency < 86 words/ minute
	Accuracy < 93%	Accuracy < 93%	Accuracy < 93%
Nonsense Word Fluency			
Phonics	Proficiency < 51 sounds/minute	Proficiency < 51 sounds/ minute	Proficiency < 51 sounds/ minute
	Accuracy < 90%	Accuracy < 90%	Accuracy < 90%
Phoneme Segmentation Fluency			
Phonemic awareness	Proficiency < 36	Proficiency < 36	Proficiency < 36
	Accuracy < 90%	Accuracy < 90%	Accuracy < 90%

Sources: Proficiency cutoff scores for oral reading fluency are based on the 25th percentile from Hasbrouk and Tindall (2005); proficiency scores for nonsense words and phoneme segmentation fluency are based on Dynamic Indicators of Basic Early Literacy Skills standards.

Early Literacy Measures - Goals and Schedule
Revised 8/20/04

Kindergarten

Measure	Fall	November	January	Spring
Letter Names/Minute	20			
Letter Sounds/Minute		7	16	36
Phonemic Segmenting and Blending Accuracy		Students must reach 12 words correct on the Blending and the Segmenting test to be considered phonemically aware.		
Nonsense Word Fluency				33

First Grade

Measure	Fall	November	January	Spring
Phonemic Segmenting and Blending Accuracy	Students must reach 12 words correct on the Blending and the Segmenting test to be considered phonemically aware.			
Nonsense Word Fluency	28	35	44	
Words Correct/Minute			20	49

Oral Reading Fluency Goals
Words Read Correct Per Minute

Revised 8/2004

GRADE	FALL	WINTER	SPRING	GROWTH RATE/ WEEK
1		20	49	1.36
2	43	72	90	1.31
3	70	91	107	1.03
4	83	101	113	0.83
5	108	128	136	0.78
6	122	139	153	0.86
7	137	148	158	
8	150*	160*		

* Temporary goals until MCA alignment data are available

Tentative Maze Goals
Correct Responses in One Minute

Revised 10/20/01

GRADE	FALL	WINTER	SPRING
5			11
6	10	11	12
7	11	12	13
8	13	14	15

Our research indicates that we will be accurate 67% of the time if we predict that eighth grade students with a score of 13.4 or more correct maze responses in a minute will pass the MTBS and eighth grade students with less than 13.4 correct maze responses in a minute will fail the test.

Note: These data were not collected using the Edformation Maze probes. Research is currently underway using these materials.

Math Applications – Tentative Goals
Correct Responses in 10 Minutes

Revised 10/20/02

GRADE	FALL	WINTER	SPRING
2	9	13	15
3	12	14	17
4	11	12	16
5	8	11	14
6	5	7	9
7			11
8			14.5

Grades 2–6 are Target scores based on passing the MCA in grades 3 & 5
Grade 7 is a 50th percentile score of all participating SCRED schools
Grade 8 is a Target score based on passing the MTBS at the 80% level

Probes for grades 6–8 are of the same difficulty level (grade 6) but are labeled
with the correct grade level for use.

Math Fact Fluency Goals
Correct Facts Per Minute

Revised 10/2003

GRADE	FALL	WINTER	SPRING
1		7	12
2	8	13	14
3	11	13	16
4	12	17	23
5	19	24	30
6	30	30	30
7	30	30	30
8	30	30	30

CURRICULUM-BASED ASSESSMENT FOR INSTRUCTIONAL DESIGN: EVIDENCE-BASED ASSESSMENT

Curriculum-based assessment for instructional design (CBA-ID; Gickling & Havertape, 1981) is a method with which student skill can be assessed using specific learning tasks. The amount of known information within a task is assessed and interpreted with the categories of frustration, instructional, or independent level. Tasks that represent an instructional level (e.g., 93% to 97% known for reading) lead to optimal student learning. Previous research found that CBA-ID leads to data that are reliable (Burns et al., 2000) and can be used for valid decision (Burns, 2004). More important, research using CBA-ID consistently leads to improved student learning.

References

CBA-ID Reliable and Valid Data

Burns, M. K. (2004a). Age as a predictor of acquisition rates as measured by curriculum-based assessment: Evidence of consistency with cognitive research. *Assessment for Effective Intervention, 29*(2), 31–38.

Burns, M. K. (2004b). Using curriculum-based assessment in the consultative process: A useful innovation or an educational fad? *Journal of Educational and Psychological Consultation, 15*, 63–78.

Burns, M. K., & Mosack, J. (2005). Criterion-referenced validity of measuring acquisition rates with curriculum-based assessment. *Journal of Psychoeducational Assessment, 25*, 216–224.

Burns, M. K., Tucker, J. A., Frame, J., Foley, S., & Hauser, A. (2000). Interscorer, alternate-form, internal consistency, and test-retest reliability of Gickling's model of curriculum-based assessment for reading. *Journal of Psychoeducational Assessment, 18*, 353–360.

Burns, M. K., VanDerHeyden, A. M., & Jiban, C. (2006). Assessing the instructional level for mathematics: A comparison of methods. *School Psychology Review, 35*, 401–418.

CBA-ID Leading to Improved Student Outcomes

Burns, M. K. (2002). Comprehensive system of assessment to intervention using curriculum-based assessments. *Intervention in School and Clinic, 38*, 8–13.

Burns, M. K. (2007). Reading at the instructional level with children identified as learning disabled: Potential implications for response to intervention. *School Psychology Quarterly.*

Burns, M. K., Dean, V. J., & Klar, S. (2004). Using curriculum-based assessment in the responsiveness to intervention diagnostic model for learning disabilities. *Assessment for Effective Intervention, 29*(3), 47–56.

Gickling, E. E., Shane, R. L., & Croskery, K. M. (1989). Developing math skills in low-achieving high school students through curriculum-based assessment. *School Psychology Review, 18*, 344–356.

Treptow, M. A., Burns, M. K., & McComas, J. J. (2007). Reading at the frustration, instructional, and independent levels: Effects on student time on task and comprehension. *School Psychology Review, 36*, 159–166.

VanDerHeyden, A. M., & Burns, M. K. (2005). Using curriculum-based assessment and curriculum-based measurement to guide elementary mathematics instruction: Effect on individual and group accountability scores. *Assessment for Effective Intervention 30*(3), 15–29.

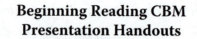

Beginning Reading CBM
Presentation Handouts

IDEAs
that Work
U.S. Office of Special
Education Programs

Student
Progress
Monitoring
studentprogress.org

Contents

Handout I: Letter Sound Fluency (LSF)—Teacher Score Sheet

Teacher: I'm going to show you some letters. You can tell me what **sound** the letters make. You may know the sound for some letters. For other letters, you may not know the sounds. If you don't know the sound a letter makes, don't worry. Okay? What's most important is that you try your best. I'll show you how this activity works. My turn first. (Refer to the practice portion of the CBM LSF sheet.) This says /b/. Your turn now. What sound does it say?

Student: /b/

Examiner: Very good. You told me what sound the letter makes. (Correction procedures are provided in the CBM LSF manual.) You're doing a really good job. Now it will be your turn. Go as quickly and carefully as you can. Remember to tell me the **sounds** the letters make. Remember just try your best. If you don't know the sounds it's okay. Trigger the stopwatch.

Score Sheet

Student's Name _____   Examiner's Initials _____

Teacher's Name _____   Date of Testing _____

School _____

Letter Sound Fluency Test

If the child does not say anything after 3 seconds: do not say anything, point to next letter. If the child names an incorrect letter: keep going. Draw a diagonal slash through any letters the student does <u>not</u> say the sound for or says the sound incorrectly. Circle the last item that child attempts. Stop at **1 minute**. If finished before 1 minute, record time.

g   l   d   i   w   n   b   t   f   k   a   p   m   j   v   x   h   o   z   y   c   e   q   s   u

_____ number of letters sounded correctly (in _____ seconds)

_____ adjusted score (if completed test in less than 1 minute)

Handout 2: Letter Sound Fluency—Student Copy

b	c	h	a

g	l	d	i	w
n	b	t	f	k
a	p	m	j	v
x	r	h	o	z
y	c	e	q	s	u

Handout 3: Word Identification Fluency—Teacher Score Sheet

Teacher: When I say, "go," I want you to read these words as quickly and correctly as you can. Start here (point to the first word) and go down the page (run your finger down the first column). If you don't know a word, skip it and try the next word. Keep reading until I say stop. Do you have any questions? Trigger the stopwatch for 1 minute.

List 16

Student's Name: _____   Examiner's Initials: _____

Student's Teacher: _____   Date: _____

Score 1 for correct response, 0 for incorrect response.

that ____	school ____	brought ____
for ____	say ____	line ____
by ____	land ____	probably ____
her ____	enough ____	close ____
up ____	live ____	table ____
them ____	against ____	strong ____
has ____	city ____	past ____
than ____	knew ____	friends ____
now ____	state ____	rest ____
water ____	wanted ____	having ____
must ____	four ____	full ____
me ____	toward ____	instead ____
come ____	move ____	case ____
still ____	power ____	worked ____
found ____	feel ____	alone ____
here ____	given ____	street ____
large ____	cat ____	Total score = _____

Handout 4: Word Identification Fluency—Student Copy

List 16

that	school	brought
for	say	line
by	land	probably
her	enough	close
up	live	table
them	against	strong
has	city	past
than	knew	friends
now	state	rest
water	wanted	having
must	four	full
me	toward	instead
come	move	case
still	power	worked
found	feel	alone
here	given	street
large	cat	

Handout 5: Passage Reading Fluency—Teacher Copy

Teacher: I want you to read this story to me. You'll have 1 minute to read. When I say "begin," start reading aloud at the top of the page. Do your best reading. If you have trouble with a word, I'll tell it to you. Do you have any questions? Begin. Trigger the timer for 1 minute.

Bubbles

One rainy day I was looking through the heavy	9
glass of the tank. I watched a school of fish swim by.	21
A big sea turtle followed them. Then I saw something	31
falling slowly through the water. It was a diver!	40
The picture shows how he was dressed. Do you	49
know what's in the basket beside him? It has food for	60
the fish.	62
The diver was feeding the fish. Suddenly, the	70
water above him became dark. He looked up.	78
Something very, very large was moving near him. My	87
eyes grew big in surprise. It was a whale! Its great	98
mouth was open as it came closer and closer.	107
"What will the diver do?" I wondered.	114
Suddenly the big mouth closed. The whale shook	122
its head up and down. Like a big dog, it rubbed	133
against the diver. He patted its nose.	140
With a turn of its tail, the big whale shot upward.	151
It swam around and around the tank. Its head was	161
turned so that only one big eye showed.	169
A young man walked up some steps to the top of	180
the tank. He bent down and called softly, "Come on,	190
Bubbles!"	191

Handout 6: Passage Reading Fluency—Student Copy

Bubbles

One rainy day I was looking through the heavy glass of the tank. I watched a school of fish swim by. A big sea turtle followed them. Then I saw something falling slowly through the water. It was a diver!

The picture shows how he was dressed. Do you know what's in the basket beside him? It has food for the fish.

The diver was feeding the fish. Suddenly, the water above him became dark. He looked up. Something very, very large was moving near him. My eyes grew big in surprise. It was a whale! Its great mouth was open as it came closer and closer.

"What will the diver do?" I wondered.

Suddenly the big mouth closed. The whale shook its head up and down. Like a big dog, it rubbed against the diver. He patted its nose.

With a turn of its tail, the big whale shot upward. It swam around and around the tank. Its head was turned so that only one big eye showed.

A young man walked up some steps to the top of the tank. He bent down and called softly, "Come on, Bubbles!"

Handout 7: Maze Fluency—Teacher Directions

The teacher says: Whenever you come to three words in parentheses and underlined, circle the word that belongs in the sentence. Choose a word even if you're not sure of the answer. When I tell you to start, pick up your pencil, turn your test over, and begin working. At the end of 2-and-a-half minutes, I'll tell you to stop working. Remember, do your best. Any questions? Start. Trigger the timer for 2.5 minutes.

Handout 8: Maze Fluency—Student Copy

SUMMER CAMP

Stuart had nice parents. They did not embarrass him in [**glad**/front/

yellow] of his friends. His father did [not/ant/**soft**] yell at him during his

baseball [center/**games**/lines], and his mother never kissed him [**in**/tot/put]

front of his friends. He generally [**liked**/flow/jeep] his parents, except for the

fact [shoe/went/**that**] they were sending him to summer [bus/dump/**camp**]

this year.

Stuart did not want [**to**/wit/cow] go to summer camp. The thought [and/

be/**of**] it made him picture himself hot [coat/rest/**and**] thirsty, hiking up a

dusty trail. [Bit/**He**/Go] knew that summer camp food had [of/**to**/my] be

bad news, too. Besides, summer [**camp**/free/dog] was for people with

nothing else [fad/**to**/sew] do. He had plenty of things planned [**for**/much/

very] his summer at home.

"Summer camp [**will**/yes/belt] be good for you," said Mother. "[Feel/

And/Lot] I don't want to hear another [catch/phone/**word**] about it!" Stuart

moped around the [beat/opens/**house**] until it was time to go. Mother [**had**/

with/boy] packed his trunk full of clothes, [**and**/sort/time] she and Dad took

Stuart to [real/glob/**the**] bus station. Stuart tried hard not [to/sun/**we**] cry

when he hugged them goodbye. [Yet/**He**/Sat] ran onto the bus and buried

[beam/**his**/neat] head in his hands. After a [**while**/tall/hate], he looked out

the window.

Handout 9: Quick Miscue Analysis—Student Copy

The examiner copy of the student reading is below. Use the blank Quick Miscue Analysis Table and write in the student miscues.

Miscue Analysis Story—Practice

<u>Adventure on Highway 66</u>	
A snowstorm could be exciting. But that much snow could cause	11
trouble. I learned it in a way I will never forget.	22
My name is John Hearon. I am a bus driver. At five o'clock one	35
morning I turned the bus onto Highway 66. It was snowing. But I was	49
used to driving at all kinds of weather. Maybe this storm wouldn't last	62
long.	63
While I drove, I counted my passengers. There was 14 – nine men,	75
four women and a little two-year-old boy. It was so early that they	91
were still asleep. No one seemed to worry about the storm.	103
But after an hour or two, I felt a wind getting stronger. That bus	117
swayed from side to side. It was snowing harder, and I had to drive more	132
slowly. I wished I had never started out. I didn't like the look of	148
things.	149

Handout 10: Quick Miscue Analysis—Practice

	Written Word	Spoken Word	Grapho-Phonetic	Syntax	Semantics
1.					
2.					
3.					
4.					
5.					
6.					
7.					
8.					
9.					
10.					
			%		

Handout 11: Quick Miscue Analysis—Practice Answers

Your miscue analysis table should look like this. Based on this table, the teacher can see that the student's problem is mistakes on short, functional words rather than content words. The teacher might choose to practice discrimination between similar words (i.e., this/that/the) and similar phrases (i.e., The big boy..., This big boy..., That big boy...). The teacher might also choose to have the student echo read and complete writing and spelling exercises for the short, functional words.

Quick Miscue Analysis Table—Practice

Quick Miscue Analysis

	Written Word	Spoken Word	Grapho-Phonetic	Syntax	Semantics
1.	can	could	no	yes	yes
2.	too	that	no	yes	yes
3.	this	it	no	yes	yes
4.	I'm	I am	no	yes	yes
5.	my	the	no	yes	yes
6.	in	at	no	yes	yes
7.	As	while	no	yes	yes
8.	were	was	no	yes	yes
9.	most of them	they	no	yes	yes
10.	the	a	no	yes	yes
			% 0%	100%	90%

CBM Resources

Deno, S.L. (1985). Curriculum-based measurement: The emerging alternative. *Exceptional Children, 52,* 219–232.

Deno, S.L., Fuchs, L.S., Marston, D., & Shin, J. (2001). Using curriculum-based measurement to establish growth standards for students with learning disabilities. *School Psychology Review, 30,* 507–524.

Deno, S.L., & Mirkin, P.K. (1977). *Data-based program modification: A manual.* Reston, VA: Council for Exceptional Children.

Fuchs, L.S. (1987). Curriculum-based measurement for instructional program development. *Teaching Exceptional Children, 20,* 42–44.

Fuchs, L.S. & Deno, S.L. (1987). Developing curriculum-based measurement systems for data-based special education problem solving. *Focus on Exceptional Children, 19,* 1–16.

Fuchs, L.S., & Deno, S.L. (1991). Paradigmatic distinctions between instructionally relevant measurement models. *Exceptional Children, 57,* 488–501.

Fuchs, L.S., & Deno, S.L. (1994). Must instructionally useful performance assessment be based in the curriculum? *Exceptional Children, 61,* 15–24.

Fuchs, L.S., Deno, S.L., & Mirkin, P.K. (1984). Effects of frequent curriculum-based measurement of evaluation on pedagogy, student achievement, and student awareness of learning. *American Educational Research Journal, 21,* 449–460.

Fuchs, L.S. & Fuchs, D. (1990). Curriculum-based assessment. In C. Reynolds & R. Kamphaus (Eds.), *Handbook of psychological and educational assessment of children (Vol. 1): Intelligence and achievement.* New York: Guilford Press.

Fuchs, L.S., & Fuchs, D. (1992). Identifying a measure for monitoring student reading progress. *School Psychology Review, 58,* 45–58.

Fuchs, L.S., & Fuchs, D. (1996). Combining performance assessment and curriculum-based measurement to strengthen instructional planning. *Learning Disabilities Research and Practice, 11,* 183–192.

Fuchs, L.S., & Fuchs, D. (1998). Treatment validity: A unifying concept for reconceptualizing the identification of learning disabilities. *Learning Disabilities Research and Practice, 13,* 204–219.

Fuchs, L.S., & Fuchs, D. (1999). Monitoring student progress toward the development of reading competence: A review of three forms of classroom-based assessment. *School Psychology Review, 28,* 659–671.

Fuchs, L.S., & Fuchs, D. (2000). Curriculum-based measurement and performance assessment. In E.S. Shapiro & T.R. Kratochwill (Eds.), *Behavioral assessment in schools: Theory, research, and clinical foundations* (2nd ed., pp. 168–201). New York: Guilford.

Fuchs, L.S., & Fuchs, D. (2002). Curriculum-based measurement: Describing competence, enhancing outcomes, evaluating treatment effects, and identifying treatment nonresponders. *Peabody Journal of Education, 77,* 64–84.

Fuchs, L.S., & Fuchs, D. (in press). Determining Adequate Yearly Progress from Kindergarten through Grade 6 with Curriculum-Based Measurement. *Assessment for Effective Instruction.*

Fuchs, L.S., Fuchs, D., & Hamlett, C.L. (1989a). Effects of alternative goal structures within curriculum-based measurement. *Exceptional Children, 55,* 429–438.

Fuchs, L.S., Fuchs, D., & Hamlett, C.L. (1989b). Effects of instrumental use of curriculum-based measurement to enhance instructional programs. *Remedial and Special Education, 10,* 43–52.

Fuchs, L.S., Fuchs, D., & Hamlett, C.L. (1990). Curriculum-based measurement: A standardized long-term goal approach to monitoring student progress. *Academic Therapy, 25,* 615–632.

Fuchs, L.S., Fuchs, D., & Hamlett, C.L. (1993). Technological advances linking the assessment of students' academic proficiency to instructional planning. *Journal of Special Education Technology, 12,* 49–62.

Fuchs, L.S., Fuchs, D., & Hamlett, C.L. (1994). Strengthening the connection between assessment and instructional planning with expert systems. *Exceptional Children, 61,* 138–146.

Fuchs, L.S., Fuchs, D., & Hamlett, C.L. (in press). Using technology to facilitate and enhance curriculum-based measurement. In K. Higgins, R. Boone, & D. Edyburn (Eds.), *The Handbook of special education technology research and practice.* Knowledge by Design, Inc.: Whitefish Bay, WI.

Fuchs, L.S., Fuchs, D., Hamlett, C.L., Phillips, N.B., & Karns, K. (1995). General educators' specialized adaptation for students with learning disabilities. *Exceptional Children, 61*, 440–459.

Fuchs, L.S., Fuchs, D., Hamlett, C.L., Phillips, N.B., Karns, K., & Dutka, S. (1997). Enhancing students' helping behavior during peer-mediated instruction with conceptual mathematical explanations. *Elementary School Journal, 97*, 223–250.

Fuchs, L.S., Fuchs, D., Hamlett, C.L., & Stecker, P.M. (1991). Effects of curriculum-based measurement and consultation on teacher planning and student achievement in mathematics operations. *American Educational Research Journal, 28*, 617-641.

Fuchs, L.S., Fuchs, D., Hamlett, C.L., Thompson, A., Roberts, P.H., Kubek, P., & Stecker, P.S. (1994). Technical features of a mathematics concepts and applications curriculum-based measurement system. *Diagnostique, 19*, 23–49.

Fuchs, L.S., Fuchs, D., Hamlett, C.L, Walz, L., & Germann, G. (1993). Formative evaluation of academic progress: How much growth can we expect? *School Psychology Review, 22*, 27–48.

Fuchs, L.S., Fuchs, D., Hosp, M., & Hamlett, C.L. (2003). The potential for diagnostic analysis within curriculum-based measurement. *Assessment for Effective Intervention, 28*, 13–22.

Fuchs, L.S., Fuchs, D., Hosp, M.K., & Jenkins, J.R. (2001). Oral reading fluency as an indicator of reading competence: A theoretical, empirical, and historical analysis. *Scientific Studies of Reading, 5*, 241–258.

Fuchs, L.S., Fuchs, D., Karns, K., Hamlett, C.L., Dutka, S., & Katzaroff, M. (2000). The importance of providing background information on the structure and scoring of performance assessments. *Applied Measurement in Education, 13*, 83–121.

Fuchs, L.S., Fuchs, D., Karns, K., Hamlett, C.L., & Katzaroff, M. (1999). Mathematics performance assessment in the classroom: Effects on teacher planning and student learning. *American Educational Research Journal, 36*, 609–646.

Fuchs, L.S., Fuchs, D., Karns, K., Hamlett, C.L., Katzaroff, M., & Dutka, S. (1997). Effects of task-focused goals on low-achieving students with and without learning disabilities. *American Educational Research Journal, 34*, 513–544.

Fuchs, D., Roberts, P.H., Fuchs, L.S., & Bowers, J. (1996). Reintegrating students with learning disabilities into the mainstream: A two-year study. *Learning Disabilities Research and Practice, 11,* 214–229.

Germann G., & Tindal, G. (1985). An application on curriculum-based assessment: The use of direct and repeated measurement. *Exceptional Children, 52,* 244–265.

Gersten, R., & Dimino, J.A. (2001). The realities of translating research into classroom practice. *Learning Disabilities Research and Practice, 16,* 120–130.

Gickling, E.E. (1981). The forgotten learner. *Nevada Public Affairs Review, 1,* 19–22.

Hutton, J.B., Dubes, R., & Muir, S. (1992). Estimating trend progress in monitoring data: A comparison of simple line-fitting methods. *School Psychology Review, 21,* 300–312.

Jenkins, J.R., Mayhall, W., Peshka, C., & Townshend, V. (1974). Using direct and daily measures to measure learning. *Journal of Learning Disabilities, 10,* 604–608.

Marston, D. (1988). The effectiveness of special education: A time-series analysis of reading performance in regular and special education settings. *The Journal of Special Education, 21,* 13–26.

Marston, D., Mirkin, P.K., & Deno, S.L. (1984). Curriculum-based measurement: An alternative to traditional screening, referral, and identification of learning disabilities of learning disabled students. *The Journal of Special Education, 18,* 109–118.

Phillips, N.B., Hamlett, C.L., Fuchs, L.S., & Fuchs, D. (1993). Combining classwide curriculum-based measurement and peer tutoring to help general educators provide adaptive education. *Learning Disabilities Research and Practice, 8,* 148–156.

Shinn, M.R. (Ed.). (1989). Curriculum-based measurement: Assessing special children. New York: Guilford Press.

Shinn, M.R., Tindal, G.A., & Stein, S. (1988). Curriculum-based measurement and the identification of mildly handicapped students: A research review. *Professional School Psychology, 3,* 69–86.

Stecker, P.M., & Fuchs, L.S. (2000). Effecting superior achievement using curriculum-based measurement. The importance of individual progress monitoring. *Learning Disabilities Research and Practice, 15,* 128–134.

Tindal, G., Wesson, C., Germann, G., Deno, S., & Mirkin, P. (1982). *A data-based special education delivery system: The Pine County Model.* (Monograph No. 19). Minneapolis: University of Minnesota, Institute for Research on Learning Disabilities.

Tucker, J. (1987). Curriculum-based assessment is not a fad. *The Collaborative Educator, 1,* 4, 10.

Wesson, C., Deno, S.L., Mirkin, P.K., Sevcik, B., Skiba, R., King, P.P., Tindal, G.A., & Maruyama, G. (1988). A causal analysis of the relationships among outgoing measurement and evaluation, structure of instruction, and student achievement. *The Journal of Special Education, 22,* 330–343.

Zeno, S.M., Ivens, S.H., Millard, R.T., & Duvvuri, R. (1995). *The educator's word frequency guide.* New York: Touchstone Applied Science Associates, Inc.

Appendix C

Forms

Student Information

Name:
Grade:
DOB:

Parent Information

Parent:
Address:
Phone:

☐ Parent ☐ Guardian
☐ Non-custodial parent ☐ Relative
☐ Foster parent ☐ Non-relative

Teacher Information

Name: _____ Best Time To Meet: _____

I contacted parents on _____ by ☐ phone ☐ letter ☐ note home ☐ e-mail ☐ at conference

Result: ☐ supports intervention ☐ other: _____

Reason for Request for Assistance: ☐ Academic ☐ Behavior ☐ Speech/Language ☐ Other: _____

Comments: _____

Student Strengths: _____

Interventions Attempted: _____

Form Completion & Turn-In Date: _____

Student Name:	Grade:	Gender: Female Male
Parent(s):	Referring Teacher:	Date of Referral:

Teacher Concern:	
Date of Initial Consultation:	Consultant:

Behaviorally Defined Problem:
Relevant Information from Cumulative File:
Relevant Information Obtained from Student:
Relevant Information Obtained from Parent(s):
Baseline Data:

Interventions Attempted Before PST Conference:
Date of PST Conferences: First _____ Second _____ Third _____
Second Intervention:
Person Responsible and Timeline:
Date of First Follow-up:
Third Intervention:
Person Responsible and Timeline
Date of Second Follow-up:
Data:

Student Name: __Trevor Sample_____

CUMULATIVE FOLDER REVIEW

HEALTH INFORMATION	PREVIOUS SCHOOLS/SERVICES
☐ Vision Concern ☐ Hearing Concern √ ADHD Spring 2004 ☐ Asthma ☐ Other Diagnosis: _____	☐ Pre-Referral Interventions – Dates: _____ ☐ Title 1– Dates: _____ ☐ SPED Eval / Services– Dates: _____ ☐ Out of District– Dates: _____ ☐ Retained– Dates: _____ ☐ Home Schooled– Dates: _____ √ Other: Good Shepard Christian School, Grades K-1, 504 plan since Kindergarten, daily point sheet

	GRADES				
	ELEMENTARY:			SECONDARY:	
ATTENDANCE		math	reading	writing	GPA: _____
# Days Absent Last Year: _____	above				Credits Earned:_____
# Days Absent Current Year: 0	meets				Other Concerns:
Other Concerns:	below				
	Other Concerns: **No Grades Received from previous School**				

INTERVIEW SUMMARY

	PARENT	STUDENT	TEACHER
DATE:	10/4/05		10/04/05
TYPE OF INTERVIEW:	**Brief ProblemSolving**		**IPF**

√ ATTACH COMPLETED INTERVIEW NOTES

CLASSROOM OBSERVATION

DATE: 10/10/05   BY: SCHOOL PSYCHOLOGIST

TYPE:	√ Interval	☐ Latency	☐ Washington
	☐ Frequency	☐ Duration	√ Other:_Ratio of Pos: Neg_____

√ ATTACH COMPLETED OBSERVATION FORM(S)

TESTING RECORDS

√ ATTACH COMPLETED WEB PORTAL STUDENT TEST DATA SUMMARY

(Be certain that all available GOM, MAP, MCA, & BST data are reported. Locate and add any missing data).

PROBLEM IDENTIFICATION SUMMARY – C1

Team Met to Review these Data on: _10/7/05_____   Prioritized Area of Concern: _Reading_____

Discrepancy Statement: _Trevor is in second grade and currently reading 4 correct words per minute with 13 errors. The target score for Fall of second grade is 43 correct words per minute.

List at least 2 sources of convergent data that support this discrepancy: ____GOM, MAP_____

√ Baseline data are plotted on the attached graph

Disposition: ☐ Level 1 Grade Level Team   ☐ Level 2: Consultation from Support Staff: _____

     √ Level 3: Problem Solving Team   ☐ Level 4: Special Education

Team Member Responsible for Follow-Up:___School Psychologist_____

Appendix D

Implementation Integrity

Tier 2 Implementation Checklist

The tier 2 intervention is:

1. implemented or supervised by a qualified teacher with reading expertise   Yes   No
2. delivered to a group of six or fewer children   Yes   No
3. implemented 3 to 5 times per week in 20- to 30-minute sessions   Yes   No
4. in addition to core reading instruction   Yes   No
5. designed to lasts at least 8 weeks   Yes   No
6. monitored with reading fluency levels and slope of student reading growth   Yes   No
7. consistent with the five areas identified by the National Reading Panel   Yes   No
8. consists of instructional methods with a sound scientific base and demonstrates at least moderate effectiveness   Yes   No

---

Problem-Solving Team (PST) Implementation Checklist

Item	Yes	No
1. The team meets on a consistent (e.g., weekly) basis.		
2. A request for assistance form (RAF) is used to identify problem and provide data before the meeting.		
3. The RAF is brief, but provides adequate information about the problem.		
4. There is documentation of consultant meeting with teacher prior to PST meeting.		
5. Baseline data are collected and presented.		
6. Data are objective and empirical.		
7. Selected interventions are research based.		
8. Selected interventions are directly linked to assessment data.		
9. The process starts with interventions that have a high probability of success.		
10. Consulting personnel assist with implementation of intervention.		
11. The team develops specific implementation plan with teacher.		
12. Parent information is discussed.		
13. Data collection plan is developed to monitor effectiveness and progress.		
14. Monitoring data are objective, empirical, and directly linked to the problem.		
15. A plan is developed to assess implementation integrity of the intervention.		
16. Follow-up consultation is scheduled between teacher and one PST member.		
17. A follow-up meeting is scheduled.		
18. A case documentation form is used to track the team's activities.		
19. The building principal or administrative designee is present at the meeting.		
20. PST members have designated roles (e.g., note taker, discussion facilitator, etc.).		

Brief Experimental Analysis—Modeling Condition—Fidelity Checklist

Mark [√] if examiner implemented step correctly.
Mark [/] if examiner did not implement step correctly.

Letter-Sound Correspondence (*Measure duration of session*)
_____ Explains procedure briefly.
_____ Has student point to letters.
_____ Models correct sounds.
_____ Signals timing of responding—e.g., by tapping finger above letter.
_____ Prompts student to respond only twice (once with instructor, once independently).
_____ Acknowledges correct responding through brief verbal praise.
_____ Repeats prompts if student has difficulty producing the correct sound.
_____ Lesson lasts approximately 5 minutes +/– 1 minute.

Decoding Words and Nonsense Words (*Measure duration of session*)
_____ Explains procedure briefly.
_____ Has student point to letters.
_____ Signals timing of responding—e.g., by tapping finger above letters.
_____ Models reading words slowly.
_____ Prompts student to read word slowly only twice (once with instructor, once independently).
_____ Models reading words quickly.
_____ Prompts student to read each word quickly only twice (once with instructor, once independently).
_____ Acknowledges correct responding through brief verbal praise.
_____ Repeats prompts if student has difficulty producing the correct sound.
_____ Lesson lasts 5 minutes (+/– 1 minute).

Brief Experimental Analysis—Incentive Condition—Fidelity Checklist

---

Mark [√] if examiner implemented step correctly.
Mark [/] if examiner did not implement step correctly.

_____ Explains that student can earn a prize *later* by reaching a certain number of correct responses during a later assessment.
_____ States goals.

Letter-Sound Correspondence (*Measure duration of session*)
_____ Explains procedure briefly.
_____ Has student point to letters.
_____ Models correct sounds.
_____ Signals timing of responding—e.g., by tapping finger above letter.
_____ Prompts student to respond only twice (once with instructor, once independently).
_____ Acknowledges correct responding through brief verbal praise.
_____ Repeats prompts if student has difficulty producing the correct sound.
_____ Lesson lasts approximately 5 minutes +/– 1 minute.

Decoding Words and Nonsense Words (*Measure duration of session*)
_____ Explains procedure briefly.
_____ Explains that student can earn a prize *later* by reaching a certain number of correct responses during later assessment.
_____ Has student point to letters.
_____ Signals timing of responding—e.g., by tapping finger above letters.
_____ Models reading word slowly.
_____ Prompts student to read word slowly only twice (once with instructor, once independently)
_____ Models reading word quickly.
_____ Prompts student to read each word quickly only twice (once with instructor, once independently).
_____ Acknowledges correct responding through brief verbal praise.
_____ Repeats prompts if student has difficulty producing the correct sound.
_____ Lesson lasts 5 minutes (+/– 1 minute).

Goal Assessment Fidelity Checklist

Mark [√] if examiner implemented step correctly.
Mark [/] if examiner did not implement step correctly.

_____ Explains to student that he or she has to beat previous score to receive a reward.

Letter Sound Fluency—Subskill Measure
_____ Reminds student of goal and prize for reaching it.
_____ Asks student to say sounds of letters.
_____ Sets timer for 1 minute.
_____ Prompts student to continue if there is a pause of 3 seconds or longer.
_____ Does not provide additional assistance.
_____ Does not provide feedback about performance during assessment.

Decoding Fluency—Subskill Measure
_____ Reminds student of goal and prize for reaching it.
_____ Asks student to read the words the best that he or she can, either by saying the sounds of the letters or reading the whole word.
_____ Asks student to point to words.
_____ Sets timer for 1 minute.
_____ Prompts student to continue if there is a pause of 3 seconds or longer.
_____ Does not provide additional assistance.
_____ Does not provide feedback about performance during assessment.

CBM—Letter Sound Fluency
_____ Reminds student of goal and prize for reaching it.
_____ Asks student to say sounds of letters.
_____ Sets timer for 1 minute.
_____ Prompts student to continue if there is a pause of 3 seconds or longer.
_____ Does not provide additional assistance.
_____ Does not provide feedback about performance during assessment.

Goal Setting with Incentive: Treatment Fidelity Checklist for Supplemental Intervention

Mark [√] if tutor implemented step correctly and/or consistently (in over 80% of instances).
Mark [N/A] if step is not needed (e.g., correction of mistake not needed if student made no mistake).
Mark [/] if tutor did not implement step correctly.

Goal Setting with Incentive: Treatment Fidelity Checklist for Supplemental Intervention (continued)

_____ Explains that after practicing it's going to be just the student's turn and that he or she can earn a prize if the goal is met in four out of the five areas.

_____ States goal for each task.

Letter-Sound Correspondence (*What sound?*)

_____ Explains procedure briefly.

_____ Has student point to letters.

_____ Acknowledges correct responding through brief verbal praise.

_____ Corrects mistakes by having student say correct sound and start line again.

Reading Sightwords (*What word?*)

_____ Explains procedure briefly.

_____ Reminds student of goal for later assessment.

_____ Has student point to words.

_____ Acknowledges correct responding through brief verbal praise.

_____ Corrects mistakes by having student say correct word and start line again.

Decoding Words (*Read it slowly. Sing it and read it.*)

_____ Explains procedure briefly.

_____ Reminds student of goal for later assessment.

_____ Has student point to letters.

_____ Makes sure student reads word slowly.

_____ Makes sure student sings and reads each word (or reads it quickly twice).

_____ Acknowledges correct responding through brief verbal praise.

_____ Corrects mistakes by having student say correct sound/word and attempt word again.

Reading Sentences

_____ Explains procedure briefly.

_____ Reminds student of goal for later assessment.

_____ Has student point to words.

_____ Acknowledges correct responding through brief verbal praise.

_____ Corrects mistakes by having student say correct sound/word and start sentence again.

Assessment

_____ Explains that student has to beat previous score on four out of five of measures to receive prize.

_____ Reminds student of prize box or shows it to student briefly.

Goal Setting with Incentive: Treatment Fidelity Checklist for Supplemental Intervention (continued)

What Sound?

_____ Reminds student of goal before starting timer.

_____ Asks student to point to each of the letters and say the sound of as many as he or she can.

_____ Reminds student to start again from the beginning if he or she reaches the end before the timer rings.

_____ Sets timer for 1 minute.

_____ Records student's response on examiner sheet (copy of PALS lesson).

_____ Does not give feedback until after timer rings.

_____ Prompts student to continue if there is a pause of 3 seconds or longer.

_____ Gives student feedback about performance and whether goal was met.

_____ Practices items that were incorrect and offers student to try to meet goal again (up to a total of three attempts).

What Word?

_____ Reminds student of goal before starting timer.

_____ Asks student to point to each of the words and read them as quickly and carefully as he or she can.

_____ Reminds student to start again from the beginning if he or she reaches the end before the timer rings.

_____ Sets timer for 1 minute.

_____ Records student's response on examiner sheet (copy of PALS lesson).

_____ Does not give feedback until after timer rings.

_____ Prompts student to continue if there is a pause of 3 seconds or longer.

_____ Gives student feedback about performance and whether goal was met.

_____ Practices items that were incorrect and offers student to try to meet goal again (up to a total of three attempts).

Reading Decodable Words

_____ Explains that student can point to each of the letters and say their sounds or read the whole word.

_____ Explains that points will be given for each sound that is read correctly, by itself or read as a whole word.

_____ Explains that extra points are given for connecting the sounds together /reading the words quickly.

_____ Reminds student of goal before starting timer.

_____ Reminds student to start again from the beginning if he or she reaches the end before the timer rings.

Goal Setting with Incentive: Treatment Fidelity Checklist for Supplemental Intervention (continued)

_____ Sets timer for 1 minute.

_____ Records student's response on examiner sheet (copy of PALS lesson).

_____ Does not give feedback until after timer rings.

_____ Prompts student to continue if there is a pause of 3 seconds or longer.

_____ Gives student feedback about performance and whether goal was met.

_____ Practices items that were incorrect and offers student to try to meet goal again (up to a total of three attempts).

Reading Sentences

_____ Explains that student has to read whole words, no points given for single sounds.

_____ Reminds student of goal before starting timer.

_____ Asks student to point to each word and read the sentence as quickly and carefully as he or she can.

_____ Reminds student to start again from the beginning if he or she reaches the end before the timer rings.

_____ Sets timer for 30 seconds (or 1 minute if more than one sentence).

_____ Records student's response on examiner sheet (copy of PALS lesson).

_____ Does not give feedback until after timer rings.

_____ Prompts student to continue if there is a pause of 3 seconds or longer.

_____ Gives student feedback about performance and whether goal was met.

_____ Practices items that were incorrect and offers student to try to meet goal again (up to a total of three attempts).

_____ Allows student to choose prize only if three out of four goals (or four out of five, if sentences were part of lesson) were met.

Modeling: Treatment Fidelity Checklist for Supplemental Intervention

Mark [√] if tutor implemented step correctly and/or consistently (in over 80% of instances).
Mark [N/A] if step is not needed (e.g., correction of mistake not needed if student made no mistake).
Mark [/] if tutor did not implement step correctly.

Letter-Sound Correspondence (*What sound?*)
_____ Explains procedure briefly.
_____ Has student point to letters.
_____ Models correct sounds.
_____ Signals timing of responding—e.g., by tapping finger above letter.
_____ Makes sure student responds only twice (once with instructor, once independently).
_____ Acknowledges correct responding through brief verbal praise.
_____ Repeats prompts if student has difficulty producing the correct sound.
_____ After practicing, asks student to do activity by her- or himself.
_____ Corrects mistakes by asking student to stop, modeling correct sound and having student start line again.

Reading Sightwords (*What word?*)
_____ Explains procedure briefly.
_____ Has student point to words.
_____ Signals timing of responding—e.g., by tapping finger above word.
_____ Models correct response.
_____ Makes sure student responds only twice (once with instructor, once independently).
_____ Acknowledges correct responding through brief verbal praise.
_____ Repeats prompts if student has difficulty producing the correct sound.
_____ After practicing, asks student to do activity by her- or himself.
_____ Corrects mistakes by asking student to stop, modeling correct word, and having student start line again.

Decoding Words (*Read it slowly. Sing it and read it.*)
_____ Explains procedure briefly.
_____ Has student point to letters.
_____ Signals timing of responding—e.g., by tapping finger above letters.
_____ Models reading word slowly.
_____ Makes sure student reads word slowly only twice (once with instructor, once independently).
_____ Models singing and reading a word quickly.
_____ Makes sure student sings and reads each word quickly only twice (once with instructor, once independently).
_____ Acknowledges correct responding through brief verbal praise.
_____ Repeats prompts if student has difficulty producing the correct sound.

Modeling: Treatment Fidelity Checklist for Supplemental Intervention (continued)

_____ After practicing, asks student to read the words by her- or himself.

_____ Corrects mistakes by asking student to stop, modeling correct word, and having student start line again.

Reading Sentences

_____ Explains procedure briefly.

_____ Has student point to words.

_____ Models words.

_____ Signals timing of responding—e.g., by tapping finger above word.

_____ Makes sure student responds only twice (once with instructor, once independently).

_____ Models reading the whole sentence.

_____ Makes sure student reads sentence only twice (with instructor, then independently).

_____ Acknowledges correct responding through brief verbal praise.

_____ Repeats prompts if student has difficulty producing the correct word.

_____ After practicing, asks student to read all the sentences by her- or himself.

_____ Corrects mistakes by asking student to stop, modeling correct word, and having student start sentence again.

Modeling + Incentive/Immediate Reinforcement: Treatment Fidelity Checklist for Supplemental Intervention

Mark [√] *if tutor implemented step correctly and/or consistently (in over 80% of instances).*

Mark [N/A] *if step is not needed (e.g., correction of mistake not needed if student made no mistake).*

Mark [/] *if tutor did not implement step correctly.*

_____ Explains that after practicing it's going to be just the student's turn and that he or she can earn a prize if the goal is met in three out of the four areas.

_____ States goal for each task.

Letter-Sound Correspondence (*What sound?*)

_____ Explains procedure briefly.

_____ Reminds student of goal for later assessment.

_____ Has student point to letters.

_____ Signals timing of responding—e.g., by tapping finger above letter.

_____ Makes sure student responds only twice (once with instructor, once independently).

_____ Acknowledges correct responding through brief verbal praise.

_____ Repeats prompts if student has difficulty producing the correct sound.

Reading Sightwords (*What word?*)

_____ Explains procedure briefly.

_____ Reminds student of goal for later assessment.

_____ Has student point to words.

_____ Signals timing of responding—e.g., by tapping finger above word.

_____ Models correct response.

_____ Makes sure student responds only twice (once with instructor, once independently).

_____ Acknowledges correct responding through brief verbal praise.

_____ Repeats prompts if student has difficulty producing the correct sound.

Decoding Words *(Read it slowly. Sing it and read it.)*

_____ Explains procedure briefly.

_____ Reminds student of goal for later assessment.

_____ Has student point to letters.

_____ Signals timing of responding—e.g., by tapping finger above letters.

_____ Models reading word slowly.

_____ Makes sure student reads word slowly only twice (once with instructor, once independently).

_____ Models singing and reading a word quickly.

_____ Makes sure student sings and reads each word quickly only twice (once with instructor, once independently).

_____ Acknowledges correct responding through brief verbal praise.

_____ Repeats prompts if student has difficulty producing the correct sound.

Modeling + Incentive/Immediate Reinforcement: Treatment Fidelity Checklist for Supplemental Intervention (continued)

Assessment

_____ Explains that student has to beat previous score on three out of four of measures to receive prize.

What sound?

_____ Reminds student of goal before starting timer.

_____ Asks student to point to each of the letters and say the sound of as many as he or she can.

_____ Sets timer for 30 seconds.

_____ Records student's response on examiner sheet (copy of PALS lesson).

_____ Does not give feedback until after timer rings.

_____ Prompts student to continue if there is a pause of 3 seconds or longer.

_____ Gives student feedback about performance and whether goal was met.

What word?

_____ Explains that student has to read whole word, no points will be given for single sounds.

_____ Reminds student of goal before starting timer.

_____ Asks student to point to each of the words and read them as quickly and carefully as he or she can.

_____ Sets timer for 30 seconds.

_____ Records student's response on examiner sheet (copy of PALS lesson).

_____ Does not give feedback until after timer rings.

_____ Prompts student to continue if there is a pause of 3 seconds or longer.

_____ Gives student feedback about performance and whether goal was met.

Reading decodable words

_____ Explains that student can point to each letter and say their sounds or read the whole word.

_____ Explains that points will be given for each sound that is read correctly, by itself or read as a whole word.

_____ Explains that extra points are given for connecting the sounds together /reading the words quickly.

_____ Reminds student of goal before starting timer.

_____ Sets timer for 30 seconds.

_____ Records student's response on examiner sheet (copy of PALS lesson).

_____ Does not give feedback until after timer rings.

_____ Prompts student to continue if there is a pause of 3 seconds or longer.

Modeling + Incentive/Immediate Reinforcement: Treatment Fidelity Checklist for Supplemental Intervention (continued)

_____ Gives student feedback about performance and whether goal was met.

_____ Allows student to choose prize only if three out of four goals were met.

Source: Petursdottir, A. G. (2006). Brief experimental analysis of early reading interventions. *Dissertation Abstracts International Section A: Humanities and Social Sciences, 67(8-A)*, pp. 2884.

Incremental Rehearsal: Implementation Fidelity Checklist

1. Identify passage used for reading	Yes	No
2. Conduct word search:		
a. Point at word and count correct if stated within 2 seconds	Yes	No
b. Every third word pointed to is easy or assumed to be known	Yes	No
3. Presented the unknown word	Yes	No
4. Ask student to state word and use it in a sentence	Yes	No
5. Present first unknown word	Yes	No
Present first known word		
Present first unknown word		
Present first known word		
Present second known word		
6. Present first unknown word	Yes	No
Present first known word		
Present second known word		
Present third known word		
7. Present first unknown word	Yes	No
Present first known word		
Present second known word		
Present third known word		
Present fourth known word		
8. Present first unknown word	Yes	No
Present first known word		
Present second known word		
Present third known word		
Present fourth known word		
Present fifth known word		
9. Present first unknown word	Yes	No
Present first known word		
Present second known word		
Present third known word		

Incremental Rehearsal: Implementation Fidelity Checklist (continued)

Present fourth known word		
Present fifth known word		
Present sixth known word		
10. Present first unknown word	Yes	No
Present first known word		
Present second known word		
Present third known word		
Present fourth known word		
Present fifth known word		
Present sixth known word		
Present seventh known word		
11. Present first unknown word	Yes	No
Present first known word		
Present second known word		
Present third known word		
Present fourth known word		
Present fifth known word		
Present sixth known word		
Present seventh known word		
Present eighth known word		
12. Present first unknown word	Yes	No
Present first known word		
Present second known word		
Present third known word		
Present fourth known word		
Present fifth known word		
Present sixth known word		
Present seventh known word		
Present eighth known word		
Present ninth known word		

Incremental Rehearsal: Implementation Fidelity Checklist (continued)

13. Previous first unknown word then treated as the first known word and a new unknown word is added	Yes	No
14. Previous ninth known word is removed	Yes	No
15. Sequence starts over	Yes	No
16. Add in new words until three errors are made	Yes	No
Total steps correctly completed:		_____/17

Appendix E: Intervention

An Intervention Template

1. **What: Name the intervention if possible or describe it thoroughly.** (For example, John will do fluency-building sessions. He will read lists of single letter and letter combination sounds. Given one minute each timing, he will try to read more sounds correctly on each of three consecutive timings. A graph will be kept showing John's first and last score on each list. A small candy prize will be given each time John reads past a predetermined score. The predetermined score will rise as John improves.)

2. **Materials: Name the materials the person working with the student will need to have in order to do the intervention.** (For example, the Morningside Phonics Fluency materials for Reading Mastery II. Use the pages that correspond with the lessons John is currently studying.)

3. **Who will do it: Name the person who will be responsible for the intervention.** (For example, Jane Doe or a substitute paraprofessional will do the intervention.)

4. **When, where, and how often it will be done: Write down the time of the day it is to be done and how many days a week. Almost all interventions demand at least three times a week in order to have an effect.** (For example, this will be done from 10:45 to 11:00 on A, C, and E days. It will be done at a desk just outside the classroom while the rest of the class is working on social studies.)

Each time an intervention is put into place, the above information should be entered on the back of the graph and referenced by date. A vertical intervention line should also be drawn on the graph at the same date.

Student: TREVOR SAMPLE   Review Date: 2/10/06

Intervention #: √ 1 ☐ 2 ☐ 3 ☐ _____

√ Attach completed, dated intervention script observation form from initial observation

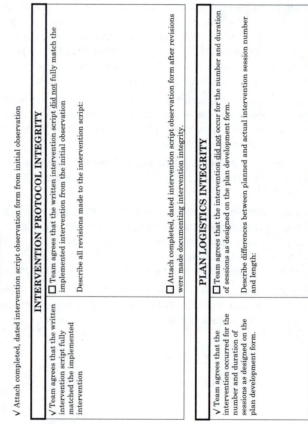

INTERVENTION PROTOCOL INTEGRITY

√ Team agrees that the written intervention script fully matched the implemented intervention	☐ Team agrees that the written intervention script <u>did not</u> fully match the implemented intervention from the initial observation Describe all revisions made to the intervention script: ☐ Attach completed, dated intervention script observation form after revisions were made documenting intervention integrity.

PLAN LOGISTICS INTEGRITY

√ Team agrees that the intervention occurred for the number and duration of sessions as designed on the plan development form.	☐ Team agrees that the intervention <u>did not</u> occur for the number and duration of sessions as designed on the plan development form. Describe differences between planned and actual intervention session number and length:

End of Year Survey for RTI

Are there any programs/materials that you are aware of that might be useful to purchase?

_____

_____

Did you use something (program/materials) that worked well that could be extended to others?

_____

_____

Is there any in-servicing that might be useful for next year?

_____

At what time of day do you think students would benefit the most from for RTI? Please give reason(s) for your choice.

   _____am   _____pm

  Why?

_____

_____

Things that I liked about RTI...

_____

_____

_____

Things I'd change...

_____

_____

_____

Additional comments/concerns

_____

_____

_____

Sample Schedule for RTI
East Coventry Elementary
Owen J. Roberts School District

TIME	GRADE K	GRADE 1	GRADE 2	GRADE 3	GRADE 4	GRADE 5
7:50-8:15	Common Planning - Monday	Common Planning - Tuesday	Common Planning - Monday	Common Planning - Friday	Common Planning - Thursday	Common Planning - Thursday
8:15-8:30	Indep. Work & Student Planning	Indep. Work & Student Planning	Indep. Work & Student Planning	Indep. Work & Student Planning	Indep. Work & Student Planning	Indep. Work & Student Planning
8:30-8:40	Opening	Opening	Opening	Opening	Opening	Opening
8:40-9:10	MATH	LA	Soc. St./Sc.	Specialist Instruction	MATH	Soc./Sc.
9:10-9:40	Tier Time *Guided Reading*	LA	LA	Specialist Instruction		Soc./Sc.
9:40-10:10	LA	LA	LA *Guided Reading Push-in*	LA	Specialist Instruction	MATH
10:10-10:40	LA/Soc./Sc.	LA	LA *Guided Reading Push-in*	LA	Specialist Instruction	
10:40-11:10	Specialist Instruction	Tier Time *Tier 1, 2, 3 Guided Reading 10:40-11:20*	LA	LA	LA 10:40-11:10	Specialist Instruction
11:10-11:40	Dismissal	Lunch 11:20-11:45	LAMS 11:20-12:00	LA	Lunch 11:10-11:45	Specialist Instruction
11:40-12:10		Recess 11:45-12:00	*Tire 1, 2, 3 Guided Reading*	Soc./Sc. 11:40-12:25	Recess 11:45-12:10	Lunch 11:45-12:10
12:10-12:40		Math 12:00-12:55	Lunch 12:00-12:25	Lunch 12:25-12:50	LAMS *Guided Reading 12:10-12:40*	Recess 12:10-12:35
12:40-1:10	Specialist Instruction 12:25-12:55		Recess 12:25-12:55	Recess 12:50-1:15	LA *Guided Reading*	LAMS *Guided Reading 12:40-1:10*
12:55-1:25	Tier Time *Guided Reading*	Specialist Instruction	MATH 12:55-1:55	MATH 1:20-2:20	LA	LA 1:10-2:55 *Guided Reading*
1:25-1:55	LA	12:55-1:55				
1:55-2:25	MATH	Tier 3 1:55-2:25 *Guided Reading*	Specialist Instruction	LAMS 2:25-2:55	Soc./Sc. 2:10-2:25	LA
2:25-2:55	LA/Soc.Sc.	Soc./Sc. 11:40-12:25				
	Pack for Dismissal	Pack for Dismissal	Pack for Dismissal	Pack for Dismissal	Pack for Dismissal	Pack for Dismissal

Appendix F

Information for Parents

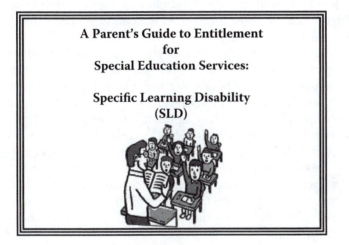

A Parent's Guide to Entitlement
for
Special Education Services:

Specific Learning Disability
(SLD)

Information for Parents

ST. CROIX RIVER EDUCATION DISTRICT
Member Districts: Chisago Lakes, East Central,
Hinckley-Finlayson, Pine City, Rush City

Kimberly Gibbons, Ph.D, Special Education Director

Introduction

The reauthorized *Individuals with Disabilities Education Act (IDEA)* was signed into law on December 3, 2004 by President George W. Bush. The revision of this law is referred to as the *Individuals with Disabilities Improvement Act*. Many aspects of the law went into effect on July 1, 2005, including changes in requirements for special education evaluations. One of the major changes of the law affects how school districts evaluate if a student qualifies for special education services for a *specific learning disability (SLD)*.

Before the change in the federal law, school districts determined that a student was eligible to receive SLD services based upon the results of a variety of tests including intellectual tests (IQ tests) and achievement tests. There were some concerns with this testing approach to determine eligibility for special education SLD services. Testing often resulted in students missing out on classroom instruction and confusion and frustration about why some students with low achievement qualify for special education services and other students do not. Most important, the results of the IQ and achievement tests do not provide any useful information for teachers to use in planning instructional programs for students.

A New Approach to Evaluation for a Specific Learning Disability

Making an entitlement (eligibility) decision for special education services for students with a possible specific learning disability involves a team process. This team, including parents, teachers, and other educators, makes decisions regarding evaluating the need for special education services. This evaluation process may result in the development of an *Individual Education Plan* (IEP) on behalf of the student, which includes specifically designed and implemented instruction, progress monitoring, and due process rights (see also the *Notice of Procedural Safeguards—Parental Rights for Special Education*). All of these components are designed to make the student more successful educationally.

Beginning with the 2005–2006 school year, the Chisago Lakes, East Central, Hinckley-Finlayson, Pine City, and Rush City School Districts, members of the St. Croix River Education District (SCRED), will use a problem-solving process that incorporates a *Response-to-Intervention* (RTI) component. Instead of looking for differences between IQ and achievement test scores, these school districts will conduct testing to determine which students are benefiting from or responding to powerful interventions designed by the team.

RTI is a method of evaluating whether a student is benefiting from a scientifically based instructional program through frequent and continuous measurement of academic performance and data-based decision making. Special education services are provided to those students who do not show adequate or desired improvement in their academic skills after receiving well-designed instruction or interventions.

The RTI process is part of the problem-solving team process currently in place in each of the member districts of the SCRED. Upon each new referral, a team of educators will complete a five-step problem-solving process. Special education decision making occurs when a student does not make adequate or desired progress or improvement after implementation of two documented, scientifically based interventions (state law requires at least two documented interventions before a special education evaluation). Solutions to instructional problems are addressed through the use of a *problem-solving model* (PSM) using the following five-step process:

1. Problem Identification. What is it that we expect the student to be able to do and what are they currently doing?
2. Problem Analysis. Why is the problem occurring?
3. Plan Development. What goals do we wish to have the student reach? What plans or steps are we going to take to help the student reach those goals? How will we measure the progress the student is making toward reaching those goals?

4. Plan Implementation. Is the plan being implemented as desired?
5. Plan Evaluation. Is the plan successful in reaching the goals established for the student?

The diagram below illustrates the relationship between the problem-solving process and an entitlement or eligibility decision for special education services for an SLD. Evaluation data collected during the problem-solving process assists teams deciding to continue with interventions or to provide special education services.

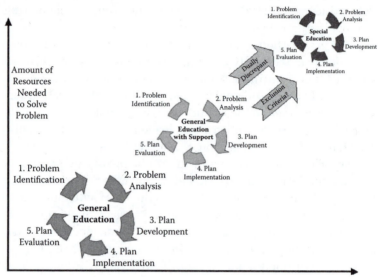

A student is considered eligible for special education services for a specific learning disability (SLD) when:

The student's academic skill level is less than desired from that of his or her grade level peers or classmates.

The student's rate of academic growth shows that he or she is not catching up to desired levels (evidence that adequate progress is not being made to "catchup" with grade-level peers).

The educational team determines the student needs special education services in order to make adequate academic progress.

The educational team also determines that the student's academic skill problems are not primarily the result of

a visual, hearing, or motor impairment
mental retardation
emotional disturbance
cultural difference
limited English proficiency
environmental or economic disadvantage
lack of scientifically based instruction in basic skill areas

Determining Success

When the IEP team determines that a student has made sufficient progress, whereby the difference between the student's performance and that of his or her grade-level peers has been decreased to an acceptable level and that the student has generalized newly acquired skills to life situations, then the student may "exit" from special education services. Exit from or discontinuation of special education services means the student no longer needs the services provided through special education. Even though the student has discontinued special education services, ongoing monitoring and plans for instructional support are made at the exit meeting.

A student's progress toward IEP goals is measured frequently to help determine when instructional changes are needed or when the student no longer needs special education services. Data from the frequent measures of academic performance is graphed to display the student's actual performance and their progress toward academic goals.

The sample graph on the following page illustrates the method of frequent measurement to determine the student's rate of progress toward reaching academic goals:

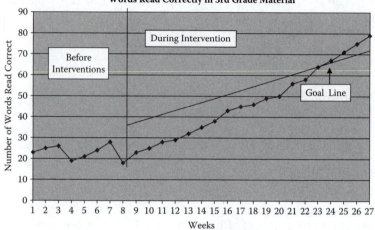

Words Read Correctly in 3rd Grade Material

KEY DEFINITIONS

Response-to-Intervention (RTI): The practice of providing high quality instruction matched to student needs and using rate of learning over time to make important decisions. Three important components of RTI are (1) high-quality instruction; (2) the slope of learning as the primary piece of information in decision making; and (3) the inclusion of a range of important educational decisions.

Problem-Solving Model (PSM): Solutions to instructional and behavioral problems are addressed by going through a five-step problem-solving model. The five steps are (1) problem identification; (2) problem analysis; (3) plan development; (4) plan implementation; and (5) plan evaluation. (See previous discussion.)

General Outcome Measures (GOMs): Quick and reliable indicators of academic performance in such areas as reading, math, and written expression.

Level: The current rate of performance on GOMs. Consider a student who was administered three reading probes and had scores of 100/5 (meaning he or she read 100 words correctly and 5 words incorrectly); 91/3; and 102/6. The median (middle) score of 100/5 would be the student's level of current performance.

Slope: The rate of growth or improvement in performance over time. In the area of reading, growth rates typically are referred to as the increase in the number of words read correctly per week. The student's weekly growth or improvement rate is calculated based on frequent (at least monthly) progress using several data points.

Dual Discrepancy: In order for students to be eligible for special education under the category of SLD, they must be different from both local norms on level of performance and slope (rate of growth)—that is, *dually discrepant.*

Target Scores: Performance on GOMs has been linked to performance on the state-mandated Minnesota Comprehensive Assessments (MCAs). This linking project has created a series of *target scores* at each grade and assessment period for a GOM such that students who are at or above the target score have around an 80–85% probability of reaching grade-level proficiency on the upcoming MCA. For example, the target score for the grade 3 winter Oral Reading Fluency measure is 91 words read correctly per minute. Students who reach this target are considered "on track" and likely to reach grade-level proficiency on the grade 3 reading MCA. Target scores have been set for fall, winter, and spring benchmark periods.

Normative Scores: These are scores that provide information about how a student performed relative to some comparison group. For example, a student who scores in the 50th percentile performed as well or better than 50% of the students in the comparison group. This score would likely be considered in the "average" range for that group. Comparison groups can range from the student's classmates to a sample of students nationwide, depending on the purpose of the assessment.

Scientifically Based Instruction/Intervention: This term is often used interchangeably with terms such as *evidence-based* or *research-based intervention*. It referes to instructional techniques, interventions, or curricula that are based on studies that (1) use empirical methods; (2) include rigorous and adequate data analyses; (3) use measurements or observational methods that provide reliable and valid data; (4) employ experimental or quasi-experimental designs; (5) are replicable, and (6) undergo a formal peer-review process.

Exclusionary Criteria: Students cannot be labeled SLD if their learning problems are primarily the result of a visual, hearing, or motor impairment, mental retardation, emotional disturbance, cultural difference, limited English proficiency, environmental or economic disadvantage, or lack of scientifically based instruction in basic skill areas.

General Education Intervention: An intervention that is delivered using regular education resources.

Sample Letters to Parents
Informational Letter

Date

Dear Parent,

The Great Valley School District believes in providing a quality education for all children. As a result, the Great Valley School District will be piloting an intervention program at Charlestown Elementary School that will provide varying degrees of support beyond that used within the core curriculum. We will refer to this support as our "Power Hour." The "Power Hour" is intended to assist all children regardless of ability. We believe in providing an avenue to reach each and every child because we know that some students learn by hearing, some by reading, some by doing, and some by watching. All of us learn differently and at different rates.

You are a vital member of your child's educational team and we encourage you to continue to be an active participant. We are planning an informational session to inform you about our "Power Hour." The first will be November 16, 2006 at 10:00 AM and the second will be that same evening at 7:00 PM. Both information sessions will be located in our cafeteria. We believe all children can be successful and it is our responsibility to assist them one child at a time. Please return the bottom of this letter to your child's homeroom teacher to let us know which information session you will be attending. If you choose to come to our evening information session, we are requesting that children not attend.

Respectfully,

Edward B. Souders

_____

Please sign and return this invitation to your child's homeroom teacher by November 14, 2006.

     ☐   I will be attending the 10:00 AM Response to Intervention Information Session on November 16, 2006

     ☐   I will be attending the 7:00 PM Response to Intervention Information Session on November 16, 2006

_____

Child's Name (Please Print)

_____   _____

Parent(s) Signature   Date

CHARLESTOWN ELEMENTARY
2060 Charlestown Road
Malvern, PA 19355

http://www.gvsd.org/charlestown

_____, 200___

Dear _____,

      We would like to invite you to an intervention team meeting to discuss _____'s progress during our "Power Hour." Your child has been working with our team and we have been utilizing different strategies and materials during the intervention time. To date, the data indicates _____ is not independently progressing at a satisfactory rate necessary to achieve long-term success.

      Since your involvement with your child's educational program increases the likelihood for success, we ask that you join us for a meeting on Monday, February 26 at 9:00 am in our conference room. During this meeting we will discuss _____'s progress and our next steps, which will include more intensive instruction and possibly a multi-disciplinary evaluation.

      If you have any questions regarding your child's areas of need that will be addressed during this meeting, please contact _____, your child's intervention team support leader.

Respectfully,

Edward B. Souders

GREAT VALLEY SCHOOL DISTRICT

CHARLESTOWN ELEMENTARY
2060 Charlestown Road
Malvern, PA 19355

http://www.gvsd.org/charlestown

(Date)

Dear Mr. and Mrs. (Parent's name),

This letter is to share with you that your child, (name of student), will be meeting daily with a member of our "Power Hour" team beginning on (Date). Our goal of having your child meet with our intervention team is to take an additional step toward remediating identified areas of need. Our team will use scientifically research-based intervention strategies and materials with (child's name) and will gather data to see if (child's name) is progressing.

If you received a letter regarding Title 1 services, those services will be provided during our "Power Hour." Please contact me or (homeroom teacher) if you have any questions about the process.

Respectfully,

Edward B. Souders

GREAT VALLEY SCHOOL DISTRICT

Appendix G

Problem Solving

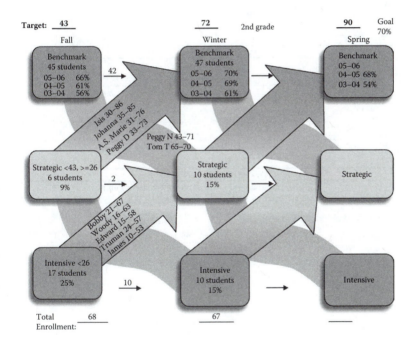

Target: _43_   _72_   2nd grade   _90_   Goal
   70%

Fall   Winter   Spring

Benchmark
45 students
05–06   66%
04–05   61%
03–04   56%

  42 →

Benchmark
47 students
05–06   70%
04–05   69%
03–04   61%

Benchmark
05–06
04–05 68%
03–04 54%

Isis 30–86
Johanna 35–85
A.S. Marie 31–76
Peggy D 33–73

Peggy N 43–71
Tom T 65–70

Strategic <43, >=26
6 students
9%

  2 →

Strategic
10 students
15%

Strategic

Bobby 21–67
Woody 16–63
Edward 15–58
Truman 24–57
James 10–53

Intensive <26
17 students
25%

  10 →

Intensive
10 students
15%

Intensive

Total   68
Enrollment: 67

195

Student: _____ Plan Development Date: _____

Intervention #: ☐1   ☐2   ☐3   ☐ _____
Area of Concern: ☐Reading ☐ Math ☐ Writing ☐ Behavior

Goal: _____
_____

INTERVENTION	
Brief Description:	
Description of Needed Materials:	
Intervention Implementor:	
When:	
Where:	
How Often:	

MEASUREMENT SYSTEM	
Data Collection System:	
Data Collector:	
What Will Be Recorded?	
Frequency of Data Collection:	
When will Data be Collected?	

DECISION MAKING RULE	
☐ Slope / Trend Analysis	☐ Consecutive Data Point Rule
☐ Level of Performance	☐ Other: _____

Intervention Start Date: _____

Review Date: _____ Time: _____ Place: _____

Student: _____Trevor Sample_____ Plan Development Date: 12/9/05

Intervention #: ☐ 1   ☐ 2   ☐ 3   ☐_____
Area of Concern:☐ Reading   ☐ Math   ☐ Writing   ☐ Behavior

Goal: _____By May 2006, when given a novel second grade reading passage, Trevor
will read 90 correct words in one minute.

INTERVENTION	
Brief Description:	**Trevor will practice letter sounds using flashcards daily. See intervention integrity check list for additional details.**
Description of Needed Materials:	**Letter cards (lower case – one letter per flashcard)**
Intervention Implementor:	**Mrs. Patience – Title 1 Teacher**
When:	**12:30-12:45, supplemental to regular reading time**
Where:	**2nd grade breakout area**
How Often:	**Daily**

MEASUREMENT SYSTEM	
Data Collection System:	**ORF of novel Grade 2 passages**
Data Collector:	**Mrs. Patience**
What Will Be Recorded?	**Words read correct/errors per minute**
Frequency of Data Collection:	**One time per week, one passage**
When will Data be Collected?	**Fridays at end of intervention session**

DECISION - MAKING RULE	
☐ Slope / Trend Analysis	☐ Consecutive Data Point Rule
☐ Level of Performance	☐ Other: _____

Intervention Start Date: 12/10/05_____

Review Date: 2/10/06   Time: 12:30   Place: 2nd grade break out area

Plan Evaluation:

Intervention #: ☐ 1   ☐ 2   ☐ 3   ☐ _____

4 Attach graph of student progress data

The current intervention began on ___12/10/05 and continued through _____2/17/06_____.

Number of data points being considered during this intervention phase? _8._

1. As a result of this intervention implementation:
    ☐ Goal was met
    ☐ Discrepancy decreased
    ☐ Discrepancy stayed the same
    ☐ Discrepancy increased

2. In the team's opinion, was the plan responsible for any change?
    ☐ Yes
    ☐ No
    ☐ Not sure

3. The next steps for the team will be to:
    ☐ Discontinue intervention – goal met
    ☐ Maintain or generalize current plan
    ☐ Select a new problem (form C1)
    ☐ Select a new hypothesis for the same problem (form C2)
    ☐ Retain current hypothesis, but modify the intervention plan (form C3)
    ☐ Consider a referral for special education

Next Meeting Date:4/28/06
(If none is needed, information should be placed in the student's cumulative record.)

Student: _____   Review Date: _____

Intervention #: ☐ 1   ☐ 2   ☐ 3   ☐ _____

☐ Attach completed, dated intervention script observation form from initial observation

INTERVENTION PROTOCOL INTEGRITY	
☐ Team agrees that the written intervention script fully matched the implemented intervention	☐ Team agrees that the written intervention script did not fully match the implemented intervention from the initial observation Describe all revisions made to the intervention script: ☐ Attach completed, dated intervention script observation form after revisions were made documenting intervention integrity.

PLAN LOGISTICS INTEGRITY	
☐ Team agrees that the intervention occurred for the number and duration of sessions as designed on the plan development form.	☐ Team agrees that the intervention did not occur for the number and duration of sessions as designed on the plan development form. Describe differences between planned and actual intervention session number and length:

Student: _____ Date Form Completed: _____

Step 1: List all hypothesis regarding cause or function of prioritized problem:	Step 2: List all relevant data to support or refute each hypothesis listed			
HYPOTHESES	R REVIEW	I INTERVIEW	O OBSERVE	T TEST
I INSTRUCTION 1. 2. 3.				
C CURRICULUM 1. 2. 3.				
E ENVIRONMENT 1. 2. 3.				
L LEARNER 1. 2. 3.				

☐ **Step 3:** Indicate selected hypothesis (circle or bold type). Selected hypothesis must have convergent data to support including quantitative data.

Student: _____

	Step 1: List all hypothesis regarding cause or function of prioritized problem:	**Step 2:** List all relevant data to support or refute each hypothesis listed **Step 3:** Indicate selected hypothesis (circle or bold type). Selected hypothesis must have convergent data to support including quantitative data.			
L LEARNER					
	HYPOTHESES	**R** **REVIEW**	**I** **INTERVIEW**	**O** **OBSERVE**	**T** **TEST**
I INSTRUCTION	Trevor demonstrates difficulty reading grade-level text because he has not yet mastered the prerequisite skills.	MAP and ORF testing both show significantly below target performance in reading (See Prob ID summary form)	Teacher reports Trevor has difficulty with letter sounds and sight words. Parents report difficulty during K-1 with reading lessons at previous school		Informal decoding test: • 51/52 letter names correct, • 21/26 letter sounds correct (missed /y/, /b/, /z/, /u/), • 5/10 CVC nonsense words, • 0/5 ccvc or cvcc words. LSF: 26 (S g K goal=36) NWF: 12 (W g 1 goal = 44)
C CURRICULUM	Trevor demonstrates difficulty reading grade-level text because he is currently being instructed at a level that is too difficult.	Trevor is currently on lesson 120 in Reading Mastery 1. He passed only 2 out of the 5 most recent checkouts due to high error rates.			
E ENVIRONMENT	Trevor demonstrates difficulty reading grade-level text because he is not consistently actively engaged with lesson content during reading class.	Previous ADHD diagnosis	Teacher reports	10/10 classroom observation: 14% passive off task compared to 5% by peers in group	

Student Name: __Trevor Sample_____

CUMULATIVE FOLDER REVIEW

HEALTH INFORMATION	PREVIOUS SCHOOLS/SERVICES
☐Vision Concern	☐ Pre-Referral Interventions – Dates: _____
☐Hearing Concern	☐ Title 1– Dates: _____
√ADHD Spring 2004	☐ SPED Eval / Services– Dates: _____
☐Asthma	☐ Out of District– Dates: _____
☐Other Diagnosis: _____	☐ Retained– Dates: _____
	☐ Home Schooled– Dates: _____
	√Other: Good Shepard Christian School, Grades K-1, 504 plan since Kindergarten, daily point sheet

	Grades				
		ELEMENTARY:			SECONDARY:
ATTENDANCE		math	reading	writing	GPA: _____
# Days Absent Last Year: _____	above				Credits Earned: _____
# Days Absent Current Year: 0	meets				Other Concerns:
Other Concerns:	below				
	Other Concerns: **No Grades Received from previous School**				

INTERVIEW SUMMARY

	PARENT	STUDENT	TEACHER
DATE:	10/4/05		10/04/05
TYPE OF INTERVIEW:	Brief Problem Solving		IPF

4 ATTACH COMPLETED INTERVIEW NOTES

CLASSROOM OBSERVATION

DATE: 10/10/05   BY: SCHOOL PSYCHOLOGIST

TYPE:	√ Interval	☐ Latency	☐ Washington
	☐Frequency	☐ Duration	√Other:__Ratio of Pos: Neg_____

4 ATTACH COMPLETED OBSERVATION FORM(S)

TESTING RECORDS

4 ATTACH COMPLETED WEB PORTAL STUDENT TEST DATA SUMMARY
(Be certain that all available GOM, MAP, MCA, & BST data are reported. Locate and add any missing data.)

PROBLEM IDENTIFICATION SUMMARY – C1

Team Met to Review these Data on: _10/7/05_____	Prioritized Area of Concern: _Reading_____

Discrepancy Statement: _Trevor is in second grade and currently reading 4 correct words per minute with 13 errors. The target score for Fall of second grade is 43 correct words per minute.

List at least 2 sources of convergent data that support this discrepancy: ____GOM, MAP_____

√ Baseline data are plotted on the attached graph

Disposition: ☐Level 1 Grade Level Team   ☐ Level 2: Consultation from Support Staff: _____

          ☐ Level 3: Problem Solving Team   ☐ Level 4: Special Education

Team Member Responsible for Follow-Up:__School

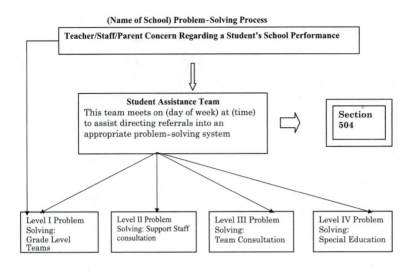

(Name of School) Problem-Solving Process

Teacher/Staff/Parent Concern Regarding a Student's School Performance

Student Assistance Team
This team meets on (day of week) at (time) to assist directing referrals into an appropriate problem-solving system

Section 504

Level I Problem Solving: Grade Level Teams

Level II Problem Solving: Support Staff consultation

Level III Problem Solving: Team Consultation

Level IV Problem Solving: Special Education

Current Organization of Building Teams

Name of Team	Student Assistance Team (SAT)	Student Support Team (SST)	Teacher Assistance Team (TAT)
Member's Names & Titles	ex. Sandy Jones 2nd Grade	ex. Sandy Jones 2nd Grade Teacher	ex. Sandy Jones 2nd Grade
Scheduled Meeting Days & Times	Tuesdays 7:45-8:45	Tuesdays 7:45-8:45	Tuesdays 7:45-8:45
Meeting Location	ex. school library	ex. school library	ex. school library
Purpose of Team			

SUPPORT STAFF CONSULTATION
PROBLEM IDENTIFICATION INTERVIEW

1. **Directional question(s):** to introduce discussion of problem:
   Ex: Describe Diane's hyperactive behavior. Let's see, you referred Johnny because of his poor self-concept, lack of progress, and rebellious behavior. Which of these do you want to start with...? Describe Johnny's rebellion (self-concept or lack of progress) in the classroom." "Are there other problem behaviors?"

Record Response(s):_____
_____
_____
_____

2. **Behavior question(s):** (Ask for as many examples as possible.)
   Ex: "What does Charles do when he is hyperactive?"
         "What does Mary do when she is disrespectful?"

Record Response(s):_____
_____
_____
_____

3. **Questions about behavior setting:**
   Ex: "When does the student do this?"
         "Where is John when he talks out?"
         "Are there other times or places when/where this occurs?"

Record Response(s):_____
_____
_____
_____

4. **Antecedent conditions question(s):**
   Ex: "What happens before Egbert begins to hit other children?"
         "What happens before Mary makes the obscene gesture to the rest of the class?"

Record Response(s):_____
_____
_____
_____

5. **Situation conditions question(s):**
   Ex: "When does Mary...Who is Mary with...What is Mary suppose to be doing when?...
         "What are the other students doing?":

Record Response(s):_____
_____
_____
_____

6. **Consequent conditions question(s):**
   Ex: "What happens after Mary...?"
         "What do the other students do after Charles climbs on the radiator?"
         "What happens when assignments are to be turned in? What happens when an assignment is late?"

Record Response(s):_____
_____
_____
_____

7. **Summarize and validate the antecedent, situation, and consequent conditions information.**

Ex: "Let's see, you said that John is able to do one-digit addition problems, but cannot do two-digit addition and no subtraction, is that correct?"
"You said Jimmy hits other children in the lunch line and, in the line for the bus, that other children usually told on him, that you reprimand him if you saw him. Did I get that right?"

Record Response(s):_____

_____

_____

8. **Behavior strength question(s):**

Ex: "About how often does Patrick refuse to do his homework?"
"How many times each day/week does Charles race about the room?"

Record Response(s):_____

_____

_____

9. **Tentative definition of goal-question(s):**

Ex: "How often would Patrick have to turn in his work in order to get along OK?"
"How frequently could Charles leave his seat without causing problems?"

Record Response(s):_____

_____

_____

10. **Assets question(s):**

Ex: "Is there something that Mary does well?"

Record Response(s):_____

_____

_____

11. **Question(s) about approach to teaching or existing procedures:**

Ex: "How long are Charles and other students doing seat work problems?"
"What kind of...?"

Record Response(s):_____

_____

_____

12. **Summarization statement and agreement question:**

Ex: "Let's see, the main problem is that Charles gets out of his seat and runs around the room during independent work assignments. He does this about 4 times each day, and...etc. Is that right?"

Record Response(s):_____

_____

_____

13. **Directional statement to introduce discussion of data recording:**

Ex: "We need some record of Sarah's completion of homework assignments--how
        often assignments are completed, what assignments are completed,...etc. This
        record will help us to determine how frequently the behavior is occurring, and it
        may give us some clues about the nature of the problem. Also the record will
        help us decide whether any plan we initiate is effective or not.

Record Response(s):_____

_____

_____

_____

14. **Questions about data recording and conditions:**

Ex: "How would it be the most convenient for you to keep a record of Charles' out of
        seat behavior?"
        "What would you record?"
        "When would you record? - How often?"

Record Response(s):_____

_____

_____

_____

15. **Summary statement and agreement question:**

Ex: "Let's see now, you'll record the number of times Danny hits other students in
        the hall. You'll record this in the morning before school and at noon, and you'll
        keep a record for one week.

Record Response(s):_____

_____

_____

_____

16. Provide *Problem Identification Summary* which is a written statement of problem
behavior, measurement procedures, and time/date for next appointment.

PROBLEM IDENTIFICATION SUMMARY

Consultant name:_____ Consultee's name:_____

Student's name:_____ Age: _____ Grade: _____ Sex: _____

Referral teacher: _____

Reason for referral: _____

_____

Problem Identification Interview (PII)

Date PII held:_____

List problem behaviors: _____

_____

List target behavior: _____

_____

Operational definition of target behavior: _____

_____

_____

Behavior Consultation Case Summary Report

What is the tentative goal?:_____

_____

Describe data collection procedure: _____

_____

Who will record?:_____

What will be recorded?:_____

_____

How often/when?:_____

SUPPORT STAFF CONSULTATION
PROBLEM ANALYSIS INTERVIEW
FOR ACADEMIC PROBLEMS

1. **Questions/statements to validate the existence of the problem:**
   Ex: "Let's look at student's progress record. What are the most difficult tasks for
   student to master?"

Record Response(s):_____

_____
_____
_____

2. **Questions/statements on current behavior and goals for behavior change:**
   Ex: "What are the expectations you have for student success in each class?"
   "What must student be able to do to improve progress?"

Record Response(s):_____

_____
_____
_____

3. **Questions on antecedent, situational, and consequent conditions:**
   Ex: "What does student do to prepare for class?"
   "What does student do during class?"
   "What was student supposed to complete during class?"

Record Response(s):_____

_____
_____
_____

4. **Summarization statement/validation question regarding target behavior and
   conditions:**
   Ex: "Student was unable to make satisfactory progress in math skills. The student
   could not complete work during class time. Is that correct?

Record Response(s):_____

_____
_____
_____

5. **Questions/statement regarding plan strategy:**
   Ex: "Perhaps student is uncertain of math facts. We could help him/her review basic
   facts. Perhaps we could encourage the student to pay closer attention to
   modeling and whole group practice time."

Record Response(s):_____

_____
_____
_____

6. **Questions/statements regarding plan tactics:**
   Ex: "How could we reinforce progress made on learning basic facts?"
   "How could we reinforce work completion?"

Record Response(s):_____

_____
_____
_____

7. **Questions about the plan:**
   Ex: "Who, what, where, when, how questions about the plan as needed."
         "What will be used as reinforcement?"

Record Response(s):_____

_____

_____

_____

8. **Summarize and validate the plan:**
   Ex: "Then we'll try this...Is that correct?

Record Response(s):_____

_____

_____

_____

9. **Questions/statements on plan implementation and support:**
   Ex: "Do you have the materials needed?"
         "Do you need assistance in getting started?"

Record Response(s):_____

_____

_____

_____

10. **Questions/statements on procedural matters, data collection, copy of plan**
    and next appointment.
    Ex: "You will continue to record...Is that right?"
          "Here is a description of the plan..."
          "When could we meet again to go over how the plan is working?"

Record Response(s):_____

_____

_____

_____

PROBLEM ANALYSIS SUMMARY

Date held: _____

What was the baseline for the target behavior?:_____

_____

Is the target behavior primarily: Skills_____   Performance _____   Both _____

What is the goal?: _____

_____

Describe the plan: _____

_____

_____

Behavior Consultation Case Summary Report

Did the consultant talk with the consultee during plan implementation?

Yes _____   No _____

If yes, describe nature, content, and duration of discussion: _____

_____

_____

Was the plan revised? Yes _____   No _____

If yes, please describe reasons for and nature of the revisions: _____

_____

_____

How confident are you that the plan was implemented correctly?

1	2	3	4	5	6	7	8	9
/	/	/	/	/	/	/	/	/

Certain it   Uncertain, have   Certain it was
was correctly   no impressions   not implemented
implemented   or data   correctly

SUPPORT STAFF CONSULTATION
PLAN EVALUATION INTERVIEW

1. **Questions about goal attainment:**
   Ex: "How did things go?"
         "Is Danny completing his work now?"
         "Were there fewer tantrums this week?"
         Note: If no, return to step one or step two.

   Record Response(s):_____
   _____
   _____
   _____

2. **Questions about plan effectiveness:**
   Ex: "Do you think the intervention was the reason for the change in behavior?"
         "What other factors may have caused the change in behavior?"
         "Could this strategy be used with another student with the similar problem?"

   Record Response(s):_____
   _____
   _____
   _____

3. **Questions/statements about plan continuation modification:**
   Ex: "How long do you think we would continue the plan?"
         "Should it continue for another week or so to see if we can reach the goal we set
         earlier?"

   Record Response(s):_____
   _____
   _____
   _____

4. **Questions/statements about continued data collection:**
   Ex: "We need to continue to monitor this behavior. Could you continue the data
         collection for a week or so after the plan is discontinued?"
         "Could you take data every other day for two weeks?"

   Record Response(s):_____
   _____
   _____
   _____

5. **Questions about maintenance strategy and tactics:**
   Ex: "One way to ensure continuation of the behavior change is fading, which means
         the reinforcement is gradually removed. How could fading be used?"

   Record Response(s):_____
   _____
   _____
   _____

6. **Questions about generalization strategy and tactics:**
   Ex: "We want to make sure the fighting is eliminated on the playground as well as
         on the bus. What could we do to promote generalization to other situations?"
         "Generalization can be promoted by self-instructions, for example having a
         nonverbal routine to go through when provoked, positive self talk. How could we
         use this strategy with Dave's fighting?"

   Record Response(s):_____
   _____
   _____
   _____

7. **Questions about other problems:**
   Ex: "Earlier you mentioned several other problems. Which of these would you like to
         work on now?" Return to step one.

Record Response(s):_____

_____

_____

8. **Procedural/termination:**
   Ex: "I'll check with you next week to see how things are going."
         "Call me if there are problems."

Record Response(s):_____

_____

_____

PLAN EVALUATION SUMMARY

Date review was held:_____

Describe data and change (if any) from baseline: _____

_____

Were the goals attained?: Yes _____ No _____ In part _____

Please describe the results: _____

_____

Was the plan responsible for any change?:

Yes _____ No _____ Not sure _____

Will the plan be continued?: Yes _____ No _____

TEAM Summary Report

If yes, please describe arrangements: _____

_____

_____

Is there a plan for maintenance and/or generalization? Yes _____ No _____

If yes, please describe: _____

_____

Did the consultee wish to work on other problem behaviors? Yes _____No _____

If yes, please describe subsequent steps:_____

_____

References

Aaron, P. G. (1997). The impending demise of the discrepancy formula. *Review of Educational Research, 67,* 461–502.

Algozzine, B. A., & Ysseldyke, J. E. (2006). *Effective instruction: A practical approach to special education for every teacher.* Thousand Oaks, CA: Corwin.

Algozzine, B. S., Ysseldyke, J. E., & Elliott, J. (1997). *Strategies and tactics for effective instruction.* Longmont, CO: Sopris West.

Algozzine, R., & Ysseldyke, J. (1992). *Strategies and tactics for effective instruction.* Longmont, CO: Sopris West.

Allen, S. J., & Graden, J. L. (2002). Best practices in collaborative problem solving for intervention design. In A. Thomas & J. Grimes (Eds.), *Best practices in school psychology* (4th ed., pp. 565–582). Bethesda, MD: National Association of School Psychologists.

Azevedo, R., & Bernard, R. M. (1995). A meta-analysis of the effects of feedback in computer-based instruction. *Journal of Educational Computing Research, 13,* 111–127.

Barnett, D. W., Daly, E. J. III, Jones, K. M., & Lentz, F. E., Jr. (2004). Empirically-based special service decisions from increasing and decreasing intensity single case designs. *Journal of Special Education, 38,* 66–79.

Batsche, G., Elliott, J., Graden, J. L., Grimes, J., Kovaleski, J. F., Prasse, D., et al. (2006*). Response to intervention: Policy considerations and implementation.* Alexandria, VA: National Association of State Directors of Special Education.

Batsche, G. M., & Knoff, H. M. (1995). Best practices in linking assessment to intervention. In A. Thomas & J. Grimes (Eds.), *Best practices in school psychology* (3rd ed., pp. 569–586). Bethesda, MD: National Association of School Psychologists.

Bear, D. R., Invernizzi, M., Templeton, S., & Johnston, F. (1996). *Words their way.* Upper Saddle River, NJ: Prentice-Hall.

Berninger, V. W., Mizokawa, D. T., & Bragg, R. (1991). Theory-based diagnosis and remediation of writing disabilities. *Journal of School Psychology, 29,* 57–79.

Bloom, B. S., Hastings, J. T., & Madaus, G. F. (1971). *Handbook on formative and summative evaluation of student learning.* New York: McGraw-Hill.

Boldt, M. (2006, June 4). Schools that work. *St. Paul Pioneer Press,* pp. A1, A10–11.

Bollman, K., Silberglitt, B., & Gibbons, K. (2007). The St. Croix River Education District model: Incorporating systems-level organization and a multi-tiered problem-solving process for intervention delivery. In S. Jimerson, M. K. Burns, & A. M. VanDerHeyden (Eds.), *Handbook of response to intervention: The science and practice of assessment and intervention* (pp. 319–330). New York: Springer.

Bradley, R., Danielson, L., & Hallahan, D. (Eds.) (2002). *Identification of learning disabilities: Research to practice.* Mahwah NJ: Erlbaum.

Bradley-Johnson, S., & Lesiak, J. L. (1989). *Problems in written expression: Assessment and remediation.* New York: Guilford.

Bryan, G., Fawson, P. C., & Reutzel, D. R. (2003). Sustained silent reading; Exploring the value of literature discussion with three non-engaged readers. *Reading Research and Instruction, 43,* 47–73.

Bunn, R., Burns, M. K., Hoffman, H. H., & Newman, C. L. (2005). Using incremental rehearsal to teach letter identification with a preschool-aged child. *Journal of Evidence Based Practice for Schools, 6,* 124–134.

Burns, M. K. (2002). Comprehensive system of assessment to intervention using curriculum-based assessments. *Intervention in School and Clinic, 38,* 8–13.

Burns, M. K. (2004). Empirical analysis of drill ratio research: Refining the instructional level for drill tasks. *Remedial and Special Education, 25,* 167–175.

Burns, M. K. (2007). RTI WILL fail, unless... *Communiqué, 35*(5), 38–40.

Burns, M. K. (2007). Reading at the instructional level with children identified as learning disabled: Potential implications for response-to-intervention. *School Psychology Quarterly, 22,* 297–313.

Burns, M. K., Appleton, J. J., & Stehouwer, J. D. (2005). Meta-analytic review of response-to-intervention research: Examining field-based and research-implemented models. *Journal of Psychoeducational Assessment, 23,* 381–394.

Burns, M. K., & Dean, V. J. (2005). Effect of drill ratios on recall and on-task behavior for children with learning and attention difficulties. *Journal of Instructional Psychology, 32,* 118–126.

Burns, M. K., Dean, V. J., & Foley, S. (2004). Preteaching unknown key words with incremental rehearsal to improve reading fluency and comprehension with children identified as reading disabled. *Journal of School Psychology, 42,* 303–314.

Burns, M. K., Deno, S. L., & Jimerson, S. R. (2007). Toward a unified response-to-intervention model. In S. R. Jimerson, M. K. Burns, & A. M. VanDerHeyden (Eds.), *Handbook of response to intervention: The science and practice of assessment and intervention.* New York: Springer.

Burns, M. K., Hall-Lande, J., Lyman, W., Rogers, C., & Tan, C. S. (2006). Tier II interventions within response-to-intervention: Components of an effective approach. *Communiqué, 35*(4), 38–40.

Burns, M. K., & Senesac, B. J. (2005). Comparison of dual discrepancy criteria for diagnosis of unresponsiveness to intervention. *Journal of School Psychology, 43,* 393–406.

Burns, M. K., Silberglitt, B., Christ, T. J., & Gibbons, K. (2007). *Comparing norm- and criterion-referenced criteria for dual discrepancy.* Manuscript submitted for publication.

Burns, M. K., & Symington, T. (2002). A meta-analysis of pre-referral intervention teams: Systemic and student outcomes. *Journal of School Psychology, 40,* 437–447.

Burns, M. K., Tucker, J. A., Frame, J., Foley, S., & Hauser, A. (2000). Interscorer, alternate-form, internal consistency, and test-retest reliability of Gickling's model of curriculum-based assessment for reading. *Journal of Psychoeducational Assessment, 18,* 353–360.

Burns, M. K., & VanDerHeyden, A. M. (2006). Using response to intervention to assess learning disabilities: Introduction to the special series. *Assessment for Effective Intervention, 32,* 3–5.

Burns, M. K., VanDerHeyden, A. M., & Boice, C. H. (in press). Best practices in delivery intensive academic interventions. In A. Thomas & J. Grimes (Eds.), *Best practices in school psychology* (5th ed.). Bethesda, MD: National Association of School Psychologists.

Burns, M. K., VanDerHeyden, A. M., & Jiban, C. (2006). Assessing the instructional level for mathematics: A comparison of methods. *School Psychology Review, 35,* 401–418.

Burns, M. K., Vanderwood, M., & Ruby, S. (2005). Evaluating the readiness of prereferral intervention teams for use in a problem-solving model: Review of three levels of research. *School Psychology Quarterly, 20,* 89–105.

Burns, M. K., & Wagner, D. (2007). *Determining an effective intervention within a brief-experimental analysis: A meta-analytic review.* Manuscript submitted for publication.

Burns, M. K., Wiley, H. I., & Viglietta, E. (in press.). Best practices in facilitating problem-solving teams. In A. Thomas & J. Grimes (Eds.), *Best practices in school psychology* (5th ed.). Bethesda, MD: National Association of School Psychologists.

Burns, M. K., & Ysseldyke, J. E. (2005). Questions about response-to-intervention implementation: Seeking answers from existing models. *California School Psychologist, 10,* 9–20.

Carroll, J. (1963). A model of school learning. *Teachers College Record, 64,* 723–733.

Christ, T. J. (2006). Short-term estimates of growth using curriculum-based measurement of oral reading fluency: Estimating standard error of the slope to construct confidence intervals. *School Psychology Review, 35,* 128–133.

Christ, T. J. (in press). Best practices in problem-analyses. In A. Thomas & J. Grimes (Eds.), *Best practices in school psychology* (5th ed.). Bethesda, MD: National Association of School Psychologists.

Christ, T. J., Burns, M. K., & Ysseldyke, J. E. (2005). Conceptual confusion within response-to-intervention vernacular: Clarifying meaningful differences. *Communiqué, 34*(3), 1, 6–8.

Clay, M. M. (1993). *Reading recovery: A guidebook for teachers in training.* Portsmouth, NH: Heinemann.

Coyne, M. D., Kameenui, E. J., & Simmons, D. C. (2001). Prevention and intervention in beginning reading: Two complex systems. *Learning Disabilities Research and Practice, 16*(2), 62–73.

D'Agostino, J. V., & Murphy, J. A. (2004). A meta-analysis of reading recovery in United States schools. *Educational Evaluation and Policy Analysis, 26*(1), 23–38.

Daly, E. J. III, & Martens, B. K. (1994). A comparison of three interventions for increasing oral reading performance: Application of the instructional hierarchy. *Journal of Applied Behavior Analysis, 27,* 459–469.

Daly, E. J. III, Witt, J. C., Martens, B. K., & Dool, E. J. (1997). A model for conducting a functional analysis of academic performance problems. *School Psychology Review, 26,* 554–574.

Deno, S. (2002). School psychologist as problem solver. In A. Thomas and J. Grimes (Eds.), *Best practices in School Psychology* (4th ed., pp. 37–56). Washington, DC: National Association of School Psychologists.

Deno, S. L. (1985). Curriculum-based measurement: The emerging alternative. *Exceptional Children, 52,* 219–232.

Deno, S. L. (2003). Developments in curriculum-based measurement. *Journal of Special Education, 37,* 184–192.

Deno, S. L., & Fuchs, L. S. (1987). Developing curriculum-based measurement systems for data-based special education problem solving. *Focus on Exceptional Children, 19*(8), 1–16.

Deno, S. L., Marston, D., Shinn, M., & Tindal, G. (1983). Oral reading fluency: A simple datum for scaling reading disability. *Topics in Learning and Learning Disabilities, 2*(4), 53–59.

Deno, S. L., Mirkin, P. K., & Chiang, B. (1982). Identifying valid measures of reading. *Exceptional Children, 49,* 36–45.

Deno, S. L., & Mirkin, P. K. (1977). *Data-based program modification: A manual.* Reston, VA: Council for Exceptional Children.

Donovan, M. S., & Cross, C. T. (2002). *Minority students in special and gifted education.* Washington, DC: National Academy Press.

Elbaum, B., Vaughn, S., Tejero, H. M., & Watson, M. S. (2000). How effective are one-to-one tutoring programs in reading for elementary students at risk for reading failure? A meta-analysis of the intervention research. *Journal of Educational Psychology, 92,* 605–619.

Ellis, A. K. (2001). *Research on educational innovations* (3rd ed.). Larchmont, NY: Eye on Education.

Englund, M. M., Luckner, A., Whaley, G. J. L., & Egeland, B. (2004). Children's achievement in early elementary school: Longitudinal effects of parental involvement, expectations, and quality of assistance. *Journal of Educational Psychology, 96,* 723–730.

Finn, C. E., Jr., Rotherham, R. A. J., & Hokansen, C. R., Jr. (Eds.) (2001). *Rethinking special education for a new century.* Washington, DC: Thomas B. Fordham Foundation and Progressive Policy Institute.

Flesch, R. (1955). *Why Johnny can't read—and what you can do about it.* New York: Harper and Brothers.

Fletcher, J. M., Coulter, W. A., Reschly, D. J., & Vaughn, S. (2004). Alternative approaches to the definition and identification of learning disabilities: Some questions and answers. *Annals of Dyslexia, 54,* 304–331.

Fletcher, J. M., Francis, D. J., Shaywitz, S. E., Lyon, G. R., Foorman, B. R., Stuebing, K. K., et al. (1998). Intelligence testing and the discrepancy model for children with learning disabilities. *Learning Disabilities Research and Practice, 13,* 186–203.

Foorman, B. R., Francis, D. J., Davidson, K. C., Harm, M. W., & Griffin, J. (2004). Variability in text features in six grade 1 basal reading programs. *Scientific Studies of Reading, 8,* 167–197.

Foorman, B. R., Francis, D. J., & Fletcher, J. M., Schatschneider, C., & Mehta, P. (1998). The role of instruction in learning to read: Preventing reading failure in at-risk children. *Journal of Educational Psychology, 90,* 37–55.

Fuchs, L., & Deno, S. (1991). Paradigmatic distinctions between instructionally relevant measurement models. *Exceptional Children, 57,* 488–500.

Fuchs, D., Fuchs, L. S., & Burish, P. (2000). Peer-assisted learning strategies: An evidence-based practice to promote reading achievement. *Learning Disabilities Research and Practice, 15,* 85–91.

Fuchs, L. S., Fuchs, D., Hamlett, C. L., & Allinder, R. (1991). The contribution of skills analysis to curriculum-based measurement in spelling. *Exceptional Children, 57,* 443–452.

Fuchs, L. S., Fuchs, D., Hosp, M. K., & Hamlett, C. L. (2003). The potential for diagnostic analysis within curriculum-based measurement. *Assessment for Effective Intervention, 28,* (3-4), 13–22.

Fuchs, D., Mock, D., Morgan, P. L., & Young, C. L. (2003). Responsiveness-to-intervention: Definitions, evidence, and implications for the learning disabilities construct. *Learning Disabilities Research and Practice, 18,* 157–171.

Fuchs, L. S. (1989). Evaluating solutions, monitoring progress, and revising intervention plans. In M. R. Shinn (Ed.), *Curriculum-based measurement: Assessing special children* (pp. 153–181). New York: Guilford.

Fuchs, L. S. (2003). Assessing intervention responsiveness: Conceptual and technical issues. *Learning Disabilities: Research and Practice, 18*, 172–186.

Fuchs, L. S., & Fuchs, D. (1986). Effects of systematic formative evaluation on student achievement: A meta-analysis. *Exceptional Children, 53*, 199–208.

Fuchs, L. S., Fuchs, D., & Maxwell, L. (1988). The validity of informal reading comprehension measures. *Remedial and Special Education, 9*, 20–28.

Fuchs, L. S., & Shinn, M. R. (1989). Writing CBM IEP objectives. In M. R. Shinn (Ed.), *Curriculum-based measurement: Assessing special children* (pp. 130–152). New York: Guilford.

Gansle, K. A., & Noell, G. H. (2007). The fundamental role of intervention implementation in assessing resistance to intervention. In S. Jimerson, M. K. Burns, & A. M. VanDerHeyden (Eds.), *Handbook of response to intervention: The science and practice of assessment and intervention,* (pp. 244–254). New York: Springer.

Gibbons, K., & Howe, K. (2000, January). The effects of monitoring student progress on grade-level material versus goal-level material. Paper presented at the symposium *Using Curriculum-Based Measurement at the National, State, and District Levels for Accountability Decisions,* Pacific Coast Research Conference, La Jolla, CA.

Gibbons, K., & Silberglitt, B. (in press). Best practices in evaluating psychoeducational services based on student outcome data. In A. Thomas & J. Grimes (Eds.), *Best practices in school psychology* (5th ed.) Bethesda, MD: National Association of School Psychologists.

Gickling, E. E., & Armstrong, D. L. (1978). Levels of instructional difficulty as related to on-task behavior, task completion, and comprehension. *Journal of Learning Disabilities, 11*, 559–566.

Good, R. H., & Jefferson, G. (1998). Contemporary perspectives on curriculum-based measurement validity. In M. R. Shinn (Ed.), *Advanced applications of curriculum-based measurement* (pp. 61–88). New York: Guilford.

Good, R. H., Simmons, D. C., & Kame'enui, E. J. (2001). The importance and decision making utility of a continuum of fluency based indicators of foundational reading skills for third-grade high-stakes outcomes. *Scientific Studies of Reading, 5,* 257–288.

Good, R. H. III, Gruba, J., & Kaminski, R. A. (2002). Best practices in using Dynamic Indicators of Basic Early Literacy Skills (DIBELS) in an outcomes-driven model. In A. Thomas & J. Grimes (Eds.), *Best practices in school psychology* (4th ed., pp. 679–700). Bethesda, MD: National Association of School Psychologists.

Graham, S., Berninger, V. W., Abbott, R. D., Abbott, S. P., & Whitaker, D. (1997). Role of mechanics in composing of elementary school students: A new methodological approach. *Journal of Educational Psychology, 89,* 170–182.

Graham, S., & Harris, K. R. (2005). Improving the writing performance of young struggling writers: Theoretical and programmatic research from the center on accelerating student learning. *Journal of Special Education, 39,* 19–33.

Gravois, T. A., & Gickling, E. E. (2002). Best practices in curriculum-based assessment. In A. Thomas & J. Grimes (Eds.), *Best practices in school psychology* (4th ed., pp. 885–898). Bethesda, MD: National Association of School Psychologists.

Greenwood, C. R., Carta, J. J., & Hall, R. V. (1988). The use of peer tutoring strategies in classroom management and educational instruction. *School Psychology Review, 17,* 258–275.

Greenwood, C. R., Carta, J. J., Kamps, D., & Delquadri, J. (1995). *Ecobehavioral Assessment System Software.* Kansas City, KS: Juniper Gardens Children's Center.

Gresham, F. M. (2002). Responsiveness to intervention: An alternative approach to the identification of learning disabilities. In R. Bradley, L. Danielson, & D. Hallahan (Eds.), *Identification of learning disabilities: Research to practice* (pp. 467–519). Mahwah NJ: Erlbaum.

Gresham, F. M., Reschly, D. J., Tilly, W. D., Fletcher, J., Burns, M. K., Christ, T., et al. (2004). Comprehensive evaluation of learning disabilities: A response to intervention perspective. *Communiqué, 33*(4), 34–35.

Griffin, A. J., Parsons, L., Burns, M. K., & VanDerHeyden, A. (2007). *Response to intervention: Research to practice.* Washington, DC: National Association of State Directors of Special Education.

Guthrie, J. W., & Springer, M. G. (2004). *A Nation at Risk* revisited: Did "wrong" reasoning result in "right" results? At what cost? *Peabody Journal of Education, 79,* 7–35.

Hale, J. B., Naglieri, J. A., Kaufman, A. S., & Kavale, K. A. (2004, Winter). Specific learning disability classification in the new Individuals with Disabilities Education Act: The danger of good ideas. *School Psychologist,* 6–13, 29.

Haring, N. G., & Eaton, M. D. (1978). Systematic instructional technology: An instructional hierarchy. In N. G. Haring, T. C. Lovitt, M. D. Eaton, & C. L. Hansen (Eds.), *The fourth R: Research in the classroom* (pp. 23–40). Columbus, OH: Merrill.

Hasbrouck, J., & Tindall, G. A. (2006). Oral reading fluency norms: An assessment tool for reading teachers. *The Reading Teacher, 59,* 636–644.

Healy, K., Vanderwood, M., & Edelson, D. (2005). Early literacy interventions for English language learners: Support for an RTI model. *The California School Psychologist, 10,* 55–64.

Heartland Area Education Agency 11 (2004). *Heartland AEA 11 annual progress report.* Johnston, IA: author. Available online at http://www.aea11.k12.ia.us/downloads/2004apr.pdf.

Howe, K. B., Scierka, B. J., Gibbons, K. A., & Silberglitt, B. (2003). A school-wide organization system for raising reading achievement using general outcome measures and evidence-based instruction: One education district's experience. *Assessment for Effective Intervention, 28,* 59–72.

Ikeda, M. J., & Gustafson, J. K. (2002). *Heartland AEA 11's problem solving process: Impact on issues related to special education.* (Research report no. 2002-01). Johnston, IA: Heartland Area Education Agency 11.

Illback, R. J., Zins, J. E., Maher, C. A., & Greenburg, R. (1990). An overview of principles and procedures of program planning and evaluation. In T. B. Gutkin and C. R. Reynolds (Eds.), *Handbook of school psychology* (2nd ed.), (pp. 799–280). New York: John Wiley & Sons.

Jenkins, J. (2003, December). Candidate measures for screening at-risk students. Paper presented at the National Research Center on Learning Disabilities Responsiveness-to-Intervention Symposium, Kansas City, MO.

Jimerson, S., Burns, M. K., & VanDerHeyden, A. M. (Eds.) (2007). *The handbook of response to intervention: The science and practice of assessment and intervention.* New York: Springer.

Joseph, L. M. (1998–99). Word boxes help children with learning disabilities identify and spell words. *Reading Teacher,*
42, 348–356.

Joseph, L. M. (2000). Developing first graders' phonemic awareness, word identification, and spelling: A comparison
of two contemporary phonic instructional approaches.
Reading Research and Instruction, 39, 160–169.

Joseph, L. M. (2002). Facilitating word recognition and spelling using word boxes and word sort phonic procedures.
School Psychology Review, 31, 122–129.

Kameenui, E. J. (2002). Executive summary of the final report
on reading first analysis. Eugene, OR: Institute for the
Development of Educational Achievement. Available
online at http://www.aimsweb.com/uploaded/files/
rfassessmentexecsummary.pdf.

Kameenui, E. J., & Simmons, D. C. (1998). Beyond effective
practice to schools as host environments: Building and
sustaining a schoolwide intervention model in beginning
reading. *Oregon School Study Council, 41*(3), 3–16.

Kaminski, R. A., & Good, R. H. III. (1996). Toward a technology
for assessing basic early literacy skills. *School Psychology*
Review, 25, 215–227.

Kavale, K. A., & Forness, S. R. (1999). Effectiveness of special
education. In C. R. Reynolds & T. B. Gutkin (Eds.), *The*
handbook of school psychology (3rd ed., pp. 984–1024).
New York: Wiley.

Knoff, H. M. (2002). Best practices in facilitating school
reform, organizational change, and strategic planning.
In A. Thomas & J. Grimes (Eds.), *Best practices in school*
psychology (4th ed., pp. 235–253). Bethesda, MD: National
Association of School Psychologists.

Kovaleski, J. F. (2003, December). *The three tier model of iden-*
tifying learning disabilities: Critical program features and
system issues. Paper presented at the National Research
Center on Learning Disabilities Responsiveness-to-Intervention Symposium, Kansas City, MO.

Kovaleski, J. F., Gickling, E. E., & Morrow, H. (1998). High ver-
sus low implementation of instructional support teams:
A case for maintaining program fidelity. *Remedial and*
Special Education, 20, 170–183.

Lau, M. Y., Sieler, J. D., Muyskens, P., Canter, A., VanKeuren,
B., & Marston, D. (2005). Perspectives on the use of the
problem-solving model from the viewpoint of a school

psychologist, administrator, and teacher from a large Midwest urban school district. *Psychology in the Schools, 43*, 117–127.

Lerner, J. W. (2002). *Learning disabilities: Theories, diagnosis, and teaching strategies* (8th ed.). Boston: Houghton Mifflin.

Levine, D. U., & Lezotte, L. W. (1990). *Unusually effective schools: A review and analysis of research and practice*, Madison, WI: National Center for Effective Schools Research and Development.

Lezotte, L. (1991). *Correlates of effective schools: The first and second generation.* Okemos, MI: Effective Schools Products.

Lezotte, L. (2001). *Revolutionary and evolutionary: The effective schools movement.* Okemos, MI: Effective Schools Products.

MacQuarrie, L. L., Tucker, J. A., Burns, M. K., & Hartman, B. (2002). Comparison of retention rates using traditional, drill sandwich, and incremental rehearsal flashcard methods. *School Psychology Review, 31*, 584–595.

Marston, D. (1989). A curriculum-based measurement approach to assessing academic performance: What it is and why do it. In M. R. Shinn (Ed.), *Curriculum-based measurement: Assessing special children* (pp. 18–78). New York: Guilford.

Marston, D., Muyskens, P., Lau, M., & Canter, A. (2003). Problem-solving model for decision making with high-incidence disabilities: The Minneapolis experience. *Learning Disabilities Research and Practice, 18*, 187–200.

McMaster, K. L., Fuchs, D., Fuchs, L. S., & Compton, D. L. (2005). Responding to nonresponders: An experimental field trial of identification and intervention methods. *Council for Exceptional Children, 71*, 445–463.

McMaster, K., & Wagner, D. (2007). Monitoring response to general education instruction. In S. Jimerson, M. K. Burns, & A. M. VanDerHeyden (Eds.), *Handbook of response to intervention: The science and practice of assessment and intervention* (pp. 223–233). New York: Springer.

McNamara, K., & Hollinger, C. (2003). Intervention-based assessment: Evaluation rates and eligibility findings. *Exceptional Children, 69*, 181–194.

National Reading Panel. (2000). *Teaching children to read: An evidence-based assessment of the scientific research literature on reading and its implications for reading instruction.* Washington, DC: U.S. Department of Health and Human Services, National Institutes of Child Health and Human Development.

Neter, J., Kutner, M. H., Nachtsheim, C. J., & Wasserman, W. (1996). *Applied linear statistical models.* Boston: McGraw-Hill.

Noell, G. H., & Gansle, K. A. (2006). Assuring the form has substance: Treatment plan implementation as the foundation of assessing response to intervention. *Assessment for Effective Intervention, 32,* 32–39.

Noell, G. H., Gresham, F. M., & Gansle, K. A. (2002). Does treatment integrity matter? A preliminary investigation of instructional implementation and mathematics performance. *Journal of Behavioral Education, 11,* 51–67.

O'Connor, R. E., Fulmer, D., Harty, K. R., & Bell, K. M. (2005). Layers of reading intervention in kindergarten through third grade: Changes in teaching and student outcomes. *Journal of Learning Disabilities, 38,* 440–455.

Peterson, K. M., & Shinn, M. R. (2002). Severe discrepancy models: Which best explains school identification practices for learning disabilities? *School Psychology Review, 31,* 459–476.

President's Commission on Excellence in Special Education (2001). *A new era: Revitalizing special education for children and their families.* Washington, DC: U.S. Department of Education.

Pressley, M. (2005). *Reading instruction that works: The case for balanced teaching* (3rd ed.). New York: Guilford.

Ravitch, D. (1999). Student performance: The national agenda in education. In M. Kanstoroom & C. E. Finn (Eds.), *New directions: Federal education policy in the twenty-first century.* Washington, DC: Thomas B. Fordham/ Manhattan Policy Institute.

Rawshorne, L. J., & Elliott, A. J. (1999). Achievement goals and intrinsic motivation: A meta-analytic review. *Personality and Social Psychology Review, 3,* 326–344.

Reschly, D. J. (2003, December). *What if LD identification changed to reflect research findings? Consequences of LD identification changes.* Paper presented at the National Research Center on Learning Disabilities Responsiveness-to-Intervention Symposium, Kansas City, MO.

Reschly, D. J., & Starkweather, A. R. (1997). *Evaluation of an alternative special education assessment and classification program in the Minneapolis Public Schools.* Minneapolis, MN: Minneapolis Public Schools.

Rosenfield, S. (1987). *Instructional consultation.* Hillsdale, NJ: Lawrence Erlbaum Associates.

Rx for Ailing (2006, June 4). Rx for ailing schools. *St. Paul Pioneer Press*, pp. A10–11.

Salvia, J., & Ysseldyke, J. E. (2001). *Assessment* (8th ed.). Boston: Houghton Mifflin.

Salvia, J., Ysseldyke, J. E., & Bolt, S. (2007). *Assessment* (10th ed.). Boston: Houghton Mifflin.

Santa, C., & Hoien, T. (1999). An assessment of Early Steps: A program for early intervention of reading problems. *Reading Research Quarterly, 34*, 54–79.

Shanahan, T. (2006). *The National Reading Panel Report: Practical advice for teachers.* Naperville, IL: Learning Point.

Shin, J., Deno, S. L., & Espin, C. (2000). Technical adequacy of MAZE probes for curriculum-based measurement of reading growth. *Journal of Special Education, 34*, 140–153.

Shinn, M. R. (1989). Identifying and defining academic problems: CBM screening and eligibility procedures. In M. R. Shinn (Ed.), *Curriculum-based measurement: Assessing special children* (pp. 90–129). New York: Guilford.

Shinn, M. R. (2002). Best practices in using curriculum-based measurement in a problem-solving model. In A. Thomas & J. Grimes (Eds.), *Best practices in school psychology* (4th ed., pp. 671–697). Bethesda, MD: National Association of School Psychologists.

Shinn, M. R., Good, R. H., Knutson, N., Tilly, W. D., & Collins, V. (1992). Curriculum-based reading fluency: A confirmatory analysis of its relation to reading. *School Psychology Review, 21*, 458–478.

Shinn, M. R., & Marston, D. (1985). Differentiating mildly handicapped, low-achieving and regular education students: A curriculum-based approach. *Remedial and Special Education, 6*, 31–45.

Shinn, M. R., Tindal, G., & Spira, D. (1987). Special education referrals as an index of teacher tolerance: Are teachers imperfect tests? *Exceptional Children, 54*, 32–40.

Shinn, M. R., Tindal, G., Spira, D., & Marston, D. (1987). Practice of learning disabilities as social policy. *Learning Disability Quarterly, 10*, 17–28.

Shinn, M. R., Tindal, G., & Stein, S. (1988). Curriculum-based assessment and the identification of mildly handicapped students: A research review. *Professional School Psychology, 3*, 69–85.

Shinn, M. R., Ysseldyke, J., Deno, S. L., & Tindal, G. (1986). A comparison of differences between students labeled learning disabled and low achieving on measures of classroom performance. *Journal of Learning Disabilities, 19*, 545–552.

Silberglitt, B., Burns, M. K., Madyun, N. H., & Lail, K. E. (2006). Relationship of reading fluency assessment data with state accountability test scores: A longitudinal comparison of grade levels, *Psychology in the Schools, 43*, 527–536.

Silberglitt, B., & Gibbons, K. A. (2005). *Establishing slope targets for use in a response to intervention model.* Rush City, MN: St. Croix River Education District.

Silberglitt, B., & Hintze, J. M. (2005). Formative assessment using CBM-R cut scores to track progress toward success on state mandated achievement tests: A comparison of methods. *Journal of Psychoeducational Assessment, 23*, 304–325.

Simos, P. G., Fletcher, J. M., Bergman, E., Breier, J. I., Foorman, B. R., Castillo, E. M., et al. (2002). Dyslexia-specific brain activation profile becomes normal following successful remedial training. *Neurology, 58,* 1203–1213.

Skinner, C. H., Hall-Johnson, K., & Skinner, A. L. (1999). Enhancing perceptions of mathematics assignments by increasing relative problem completion rates through the interspersal technique. *Journal of Experimental Education, 68*, 43–59.

Snow, C. E., Burns, M. S., & Griffin, P. (Eds.) (1998). *Preventing reading difficulties in young children.* Washington, DC: National Academies Press.

Sornson, R., Frost, F., & Burns, M. (2005). Instructional support teams in Michigan: Data from Northville Public Schools. *Communiqué, 33*(5), 28–29.

Speece, D. L, & Case, L. P. (2001). Classification in context: An alternative approach to identifying early reading disability. *Journal of Educational Psychology, 93*, 735–749.

Speece, D. L., Case, L. P., & Molloy, D. E. (2003). Responsiveness to general education instruction as the first gate to learning disabilities identification. *Learning Disabilities Research and Practice, 18*, 147–156.

Stein, M., Johnson, B., & Gutlohn, L. (1999). Analyzing beginning reading programs: The relationship between decoding instruction and text. *Remedial and Special Education, 20*, 275–287.

Sugai, G., & Horner, R. H. (1999). Discipline and behavioral support: Practices, pitfalls, and promises. *Effective School Practices, 17*(4), 10–22.

Swanson, H. L. (1999). Instructional components that predict treatment outcomes for students with learning disabilities: Support for a combined strategy and direct instruction model. *Learning Disabilities Research and Practice, 14*, 129–140.

Swanson, H. L., Hoskyn, M., & Lee, C. (1999). *Interventions for students with learning disabilities: A meta-analysis of treatment outcomes.* New York: Guilford.

Sylwester, M. (2006, June 4). Analysis reveals true performance. *St. Paul Pioneer Press*, p. A10.

Taylor, B. M., Frye, B. J., & Maruyama, G. M. (1990). Time spent reading and reading growth. *American Educational Research Journal, 27*, 351–362.

Taylor, B. M., Pearson, P. D., Clark, K., & Walpole, S. (2000). Effective schools and accomplished teachers: Lessons about primary-grade reading instruction in low-income schools. *Elementary School Journal, 101*, 121–165.

Thelen, R. L., Burns, M. K., & Christiansen, N. D. (2004). Effects of high-incidence disability labels on the expectations of teachers, peers, and adults not in education. *Ethical Human Sciences and Services, 5*, 183–194.

Tilly, W. D. (2002). Best practices in school psychology as a problem-solving enterprise. In A. Thomas & J. Grimes (Eds.), *Best practices in school psychology* (4th ed., pp. 21–36). Bethesda, MD: National Association of School Psychologists.

Tilly, W. D. (2003, December). *How many tiers are needed for successful prevention and early intervention? Heartland Area Education Agency's evolution from four to three tiers.* Paper presented at the National Research Center on Learning Disabilities Responsiveness-to-Intervention Symposium, Kansas City, MO.

Topping, K. J., Samuels, J., & Paul, T. (2007). Does practice make perfect? Independent reading quantity, quality, and student achievement. *Learning and Instruction, 17*, 253–264.

Torgesen, J. K., Alexander, A. W., Wagner, R. K., Rashotte, C. A., Voeller, K. K. S., & Conway, T. (2001). Intensive remedial instruction for children with severe reading disabilities: Immediate and long-term outcomes for two instructional approaches. *Journal of Learning Disabilities, 34*, 33–58.

Treptow, M. A., Burns, M. K., & McComas, J. J. (2007). Reading at the frustration, instructional, and independent levels: Effects on student time on task and comprehension. *School Psychology Review, 36*, 159–166.

Tucker, J. A. (1989). *Basic flashcard technique when vocabulary is the goal.* Unpublished teaching materials, School of Education, University of Chattanooga, Chattanooga, TN.

Upah, K. R., & Tilly, W. D (2002), Best practices in designing, implementing, and evaluating quality interventions. In A. Thomas & J. Grimes (Eds.), *Best practices in school psychology* (4th ed., pp. 483–502). Bethesda, MD: National Association of School Psychologists.

U.S. Department of Education (1983). *A nation at risk: The imperative for school reform.* Washington, DC: Author.

U.S. Department of Education (2002). *Twenty-fourth annual report to Congress on the implementation of the Individuals with Disabilities Education Act.* Washington, DC: U.S. Government Printing Office.

U.S. Senate Committee on Appropriations (1997). *Congressional charge to the National Reading Panel: Senate report 105-58.* Washington, DC: author.

VanDerHeyden, A. M., & Burns, M. K. (2005). Using curriculum-based assessment and curriculum-based measurement to guide elementary mathematics instruction: Effect on individual and group accountability scores. *Assessment for Effective Intervention 30*(3), 15–29.

VanDerHeyden, A. M., Witt, J. C., & Naquin, G. (2003). Development and validation of a process for screening referrals to special education. *School Psychology Review, 32*, 204–227.

Vanderwood, M. L., & Nam, J. E. (2007). Response to intervention for English language learners: Current development and future directions. In S. Jimerson, M. K. Burns, & A. M. VanDerHeyden (Eds.), *Handbook of response to intervention: The science and practice of assessment and intervention* (pp. 408–417). New York: Springer.

Vaughn, S., & Fuchs, L. S. (2003). Redefining learning disabilities as inadequate response to instruction: The promise and potential problems. *Learning Disabilities Research and Practice, 18,* 137–146.

Vaughn, S., Gersten, R., & Chard, D. J. (2000). The underlying message in LD intervention research: Findings from research syntheses. *Exceptional Children, 67,* 99–114.

Vaughn, S., Wanzek, J., Linan-Thompson, S., Murray, C. (2007). Monitoring response to supplemental services for students at risk for reading difficulties: High and low responders. In S. Jimerson, M. K. Burns, & A. M. VanDerHeyden (Eds.), *Handbook of response to intervention: The science and practice of assessment and intervention* (pp. 234–243). New York: Springer.

William, D. (2006). Formative assessment: Getting the focus right. *Educational Assessment, 11,* 283–289.

Windram, H., Scierka, B., & Silberglitt, B. (2007). Response to intervention at the secondary level: A description of two districts' models of implementation. *Communique, 35*(5), 43–45.

Winne, P. H., & Marx, R. W. (1982). Students' and teachers' views of thing processes for classroom learning. *Elementary School Journal, 82,* 493–518.

Wong, K. K., Guthrie, J. W., & Harris, D. N. (2004). Guest editors' preface to the special series. *Peabody Journal of Education, 79,* 1–6.

Ysseldyke, J., & Algozzine, R. (1995). *Special education: A practical approach for teachers* (3rd ed.) Boston: Houghton Mifflin.

Ysseldyke, J. E. (2005). Assessment and decision making for students with learning disabilities: What if this is as good as it gets? *Learning Disability Quarterly, 28,* 125–128.

Ysseldyke, J. E., & Burns, M. K. (in press). Functional assessment of instructional environments for the purpose of making data-driven instructional decisions. In C. Reynolds & T. B. Gutkin (Eds.), *The handbook of school psychology* (4th ed.). New York: Wiley.

Ysseldyke, J. E., & Christenson, S. L. (2002). *FAAB: Functional assessment of academic behavior: Creating successful learning environments.* Longmont, CO: Sopris West.

Index

CD Contents:
Practical Resources

A Short Introduction to RTI—Power Point Presentation

Assessment
    Assessment Instruments and Cut Scores for Reading Problem Analysis
    2004 Early Literacy Measures, Schedule, and Goals from SCRED
    2004 Reading Fluency Goals from SCRED
    2004 MAZE Goals from SCRED
    2004 Math Application Goals from SCRED
    2004 Math Fact Goals from SCRED
    CBA-ID as an Evidence-Based Assessment
    CBM Training Handout from the National Institute for Progress Monitoring
    Sample Reading Fluency Data File in MS Excel

Forms
    Request for Assistance Form
    Request for Assistance Form 2
    Problem Identification Screening Summary
    Problem Identification Screening Summary Sample

Implementation Integrity
    Tier 2 Implementation Checklist
    Problem-Solving Team Implementation Checklist
    Sample BEA Implementation Checklist
    Sample Incremental Rehearsal Implementation Checklist

Intervention
    Intervention Design Template
    Sample Intervention Protocol
    Steps for Incremental Rehearsal
    Sample Tier 2 Schedule
    Standard Protocol Intervention Documentation Form

Information for Parents
  Sample Parent Brochure for R-T-I
  Sample Parent Letter
  Sample Parent Notification Letter
  Sample Parent Invitation Letter

Problem Solving
  Chutes and Ladders Chart
  Sample Plan Development Form
  Plan Development Example
  Sample Plan Evaluation Form
  Sample Plan Implementation Form
  Sample Problem Analysis Form
  Problem Analysis Example
  Problem Identification Example
  Problem-Solving Team Planning Process
  Problem-Solving Team Planning Process Example
  Problem Identification Interview